ENCOUNTERING GOD

*Joy and healing through meeting with
your heavenly Father*

Tracy Williamson

New Wine Press

New Wine Ministries
PO Box 17
Chichester
West Sussex
United Kingdom
PO19 2AW

Scripture quotations are taken from the following version of the Bible:
NIV – The Holy Bible, New International Version. Copyright © 1973, 1978, 1984 by International Bible Society. Used by permission of Hodder and Stoughton Limited.
NLT – *Holy Bible, New Living Translation* copyright © 1996 by Tyndale Charitable Trust. Used by permission of Tyndale House Publishers.

All stories in this book are true and as accurate as possible. If there are any minor details that are incorrect it is accidental and I apologise. For the sake of confidentiality I have not always given people's real names.

ISBN 978–1–903725–93–1

Typeset by CRB Associates, Reepham, Norfolk
Cover design by CCD, www.ccdgroup.co.uk
Printed in Malta

CONTENTS

Dedication   4

Acknowledgements   5

Foreword   6

Introduction   8

Chapter 1   Hunger   13

Chapter 2   The Skeleton Key of Trust   27

Chapter 3   The Tap On The Shoulder   41

Chapter 4   Life Changing Dialogue   53

Chapter 5   Learning God's Language   73

About the Author   92

DEDICATION

I would like to dedicate this book to Chelsea – may you find the joy you long for in knowing how deeply loved and precious you are to Father God and may you discover how much He delights to be with you, sharing His heart of love with you.

And to all who long to know God's love in their hearts, not just in their heads.

ACKNOWLEDGEMENTS

Thanks so much to all of you dear friends and prayer supporters who have believed in me and carried on praying for this book to come about even when there was no sign of it being written! It is through your prayers I have experienced God drawing close to me in new ways and have been enabled to write this book with a real joy and thankfulness.

Thanks to the many people whose lives and experience of God have moved and challenged me deeply. Some of you are dear friends; others I have never met but you have impacted me through your books or sermons. Thank you all for the way you have inspired me.

Thanks to Lilian, Diana, Chris and many others whose stories I have used in this book. Thank you for your willingness for others to share and be blessed by your experiences of God.

Thanks to Mags, my spiritual director at Loyola Hall for the last two years. You have taught me so much how I can meet with God and experience His joy and healing.

Thanks to Marilyn, you are a wonderful friend, colleague and inspiration, and have been so supportive in the writing of this book.

Most of all, thank You Father, Son and Holy Spirit, that all of this has only come about because of You and through Your empowering love.

FOREWORD

Reading an author's unpublished manuscript is always a privilege, I find. Reading the manuscript of *this* book before it was published was an extra-special privilege for a whole variety of reasons.

One reason is that I have known the author for many years, but had no idea that God had entrusted her with the gift of writing that has engaged and thrilled me as I have feasted on the powerfully penned pages of this inspired book. Another reason why I felt so privileged to read the manuscript of *this* book is that I found myself filled with awe as page after page revealed ways in which Tracy's relationship with God has deepened over the years.

That is not to say that *Encountering God* is an autobiography. Rather, it is a powerful, persuasive, appetising testimony that people who yearn for a closer walk with God will, I believe, treasure and refer to over and over again.

Using humility and sincerity, integrity and gratitude as well as humour, Tracy reflects with great gratitude on the way God has guided her along life's paths. The result has been that her relationship with God has gone deeper and deeper over the years.

Certain that God wants each of us to be on the receiving end of His goodness, grace and love as well as to go steadily deeper into that love, with characteristic joy, enthusiasm and yearning, Tracy decided to share with others "tips for the journey" where every footstep can carry us closer to God.

The result is that this is not a book to be read once and then placed on a book-shelf to gather dust. It is a book to relish, read, re-read and pray with; a book that brings glory to the God it describes. Within these pages we watch Jesus enjoying His times of prayer with His Father. We are provided with ways in which we may helpfully and prayerfully engage with Scripture, and we are reminded that we can never have enough of God.

Having whetted our appetite with such claims, Tracy provides us with exercises to engage in prayerfully: exercises that could change the lives and deepen the prayer experience of those who engage in them. In other words, reading and responding to the challenges of this moving book could draw the reader closer and closer to God: Father, Son and Holy Spirit.

Joyce Huggett

INTRODUCTION

"This is where I want you to go."

I was startled. Where had this come from? Surely this couldn't be God speaking? I shook my head and dismissed that idea. I was in the middle of a conversation with a lady I'd never met before and needed to concentrate.

It was late in the evening in a cold church and I felt ready for bed! I work with the blind singer/songwriter Marilyn Baker and we had just finished doing a concert there. Several people had thanked us or asked for prayer but now the church was nearly empty. Then a lady sat down, obviously wanting to talk. I sighed inwardly as she began sharing excitedly and at length. Being severely deaf I don't hear conversation and am dependent on Marilyn translating to me in the special deaf/blind finger spelling we use, but at the end of a long day tiredness can get in the way of success! This was one of those days but the lady's enthusiasm was infectious so I struggled to follow Marilyn's hands.

I missed most of it but a few phrases "nabbed" me: "retreat"; "five weeks"; "silent"; "fell in love with God"; "totally changed my life . . . " It was obvious she was describing some deep and meaningful experience of God. Although I couldn't hear her words I could see such a glow of love and joy in her face and felt impressed by the reality of whatever that experience had been. I found myself longing to have such a reality of God in my own life. It was then that the thought came into my mind: "This is where I want you to go." I laughed! After all, I didn't even know if she'd been anywhere or just had an experience of God at home. I was obviously ready for bed!

But the thought stayed in my mind through that night. Was God trying to communicate with me? I didn't know what to think. I'd tried asking Marilyn for more detail once we got back to our hosts but Marilyn was tired too. She'd tried to translate a lot of conversations to me that night and felt muddled. It was too late now, the lady had gone, I must have been imagining things.

I was astonished, therefore, the next morning when there was a knock at the door and that same lady was ushered in. "I heard you were free today," she smiled, "and I knew Tracy wanted to hear about my retreat, so I've brought round some stuff to show her!"

How had she known? Could Marilyn have indicated I was interested? Yet Marilyn didn't know that thought had passed my mind. I was amazed but as I began to talk with her I realized that it was indeed God at work.

Carole had just returned from a five-week silent retreat held in a Jesuit retreat centre called Loyola Hall near Liverpool. The experience had changed her life and made her relationship with God more real than ever before. I had never heard of Loyola Hall or silent retreats or Jesuit centres. Coming from a charismatic background, all such concepts were alien to me, yet as she spoke, I became more and more certain that this was where God wanted me to go. It was a strange experience because a big part of me wanted to run away from the idea! Yet I felt a longing to experience the reality of God for myself. I had a short sabbatical planned for later that year and had thought of going abroad or joining some other ministry, but nothing had worked out.

Was this really what God wanted me to do?

The upshot of that experience was that I did indeed go to Loyola Hall for part of my sabbatical and have subsequently been back twice more. Carole's had been five weeks duration but an eight day retreat was more suitable for me and fitted with my dates. I did not know what to expect but those eight days proved to be truly life changing. I have learnt to meet with my Father God, communicate with Him and hear His voice in a deeper way than ever before.

The amazing thing is that God took the initiative to direct me to Loyola Hall in the first place. I wasn't expecting Him to speak personally at that particular moment; I was tired and cold and wanting my bed! Yet He knew that I longed to know Him more deeply and also needed to know how to best use my sabbatical. He had heard my prayers and answered by putting that thought into my mind: "This is where I want you to go." That was just the beginning.

Since then, a deeper and deeper awareness has grown in me that God our Father wants to communicate with us, to draw us into a new understanding of His love and the power of what Jesus did for us on the cross, and to fill us with His Spirit in such a way that we are healed and transformed and reflect His beauty and loveliness to those around us.

At the retreat centres they refer to our relationship with God as being on a journey. This journey takes our whole lifetime. The end of it is more exciting than we can possibly imagine but the journey itself is also the most dynamic of adventures. The reason is that, incredibly, God travels it with us as well as meeting us at the end! And the journey is a hide-and-seek game of discovering Him at any moment. Whether we are riding up to the top of a mountain or passing through a dark tunnel, He is alongside and wanting to share it with us and show us incredible things that we would not have seen on our own. We may be resting in a peaceful lay-by or have traffic hurtling in all directions in a frenzied city. He's there

too and wants to hear us say "Wow! You are here!" The most
dynamic thing is that each time we encounter Him He
changes us! And each time He changes us we find more and
more of the load we've been carrying is gone because He is
carrying it for us.

As someone who spends my whole life travelling, I know the
joy of unexpected reunions. A friendly face suddenly recognised in the middle of a concert ignites the whole event with
happy anticipation. This is the joy we experience when we
encounter God on our life journey.

I also know the importance of packing the right things to
take with me. Once I forgot to take any underwear for a whole
week's conference! At the time it wasn't so funny!

God has given us a suitcase of vital accessories to take and
use on our journey with Him. We need to open the case and use
and wear what's inside! Each item helps us to recognise Him,
see Him, hear Him, be filled with Him and receive the healing,
transforming love He gives us. Each item helps us get a bit
further along the road.

This book is a fellow traveller's guide to discovering and
using some of those accessories. Each chapter's teaching
centres around a key aspect of our relationship with God
and how we can develop life-changing encounters with Him.
The stories and exercises throughout inspire us, they are
traveller tips for the journey.

It's not a journey that I've reached the end of yet. If I had I
wouldn't be writing this book! I've still a long way to go and
you are probably further along the path than I am! But every
step of the journey counts because He is with me and I want
to take hold of all He wants to show me on the way. I want to
know the joy of suddenly encountering Him, hearing His life
changing words and being transformed into His likeness.

He wants *you* to know that same life-changing joy. May this book inspire and help you on your journey!

Tracy Williamson
February 2007

CHAPTER 1

HUNGER

"This is the air I breathe, this is the air I breathe, your Holy presence living in me. This is my daily bread, this is my daily bread, your very word spoken to me. And I, I'm desperate for you. And I, I'm lost without you."[1]

THE MOST IMPORTANT BIT OF LUGGAGE!

When Marilyn and I travel around there is one thing that always ranks as the most vital bit of equipment. Not concert clothes, jewellery, cosmetics or keyboards. All these things are important but pale into insignificance against our need to take some food!

Sandwiches, fruit, chocolate. These are all good antidotes to the pangs of hunger and we are soon easily filled.

More difficult to satisfy is the hunger and longing for "something" that we all feel deep inside us. Many of us never even admit it, but as the disciples found, it is in acknowledging it that we find the answer.

One day they watched Jesus praying. There was something different about it to the way other religious leaders prayed. Not just because of words and methods but with what they could see happening between Jesus and God. Jesus was enjoying His prayer time. Something real was taking place: connection … communication … peace and power. Jesus transformed before their eyes, a frightening yet wonderful reality. The more of this they witnessed, the deeper the hunger within them. They wanted that reality of enjoying God themselves. But was that even possible?

WE ARE HUNGRY

I was at a church evangelistic rally on the night I publicly gave my life to Jesus. Around me other students from my college were praying and worshipping. As I looked at their faces I could see something real was happening. These were people I knew and mixed with every day but this was a new dimension. There was a joy in their expressions; they were communicating with someone they really wanted to be with, a very special friend. It filled me with awe and a hunger to experience this same joy in my own life. It was seeing my friends in prayer and worship which took me to the front to publicly give my life to God.

Many of us are also hungry for a prayer life that is real. We see the power and effectiveness of Jesus' prayers or the ability of others to pray and spend time with God and we long for that same effectiveness in our own lives. We may go to one church after another or attend every possible conference trying to find the teaching that will impact and empower us. We set our alarm clocks for an early hour yet find our minds zigzagging to our day's tasks or we just drift back to sleep! Condemnation then sets in and we feel we have failed yet again. The reality of experiencing powerful, effective prayer seems an elusive dream.

Have you ever considered that you may be trying too hard?

One of the most effective prayers of the Bible is that recorded when one of the disciples, maybe more daring than the rest, put his hunger into words: *"Lord, teach us to pray"* (Luke 11:1).

We probably would not even consider that a prayer. It was just a verbal request, a moment of conversation between Jesus and a friend. Yet that is exactly what prayer is. It is real communication between two people who know and trust each other and enjoy each other's company. While one shares the other listens, knowing that his turn will also come to share and be listened to.

This request was one that Jesus really delighted in answering. He loved talking with His Father more than anything else and rejoiced that the disciples were recognising that delight and wanting to know it for themselves. His answer took them completely out of the realm of ornate prayer to a God of judgement into the place of relationship with a Father who is personal and approachable, albeit holy and powerful.

Prayer is Relationship with a Father

"Our Father in Heaven, hallowed be your name."

(Matthew 6:9)

This response stunned the disciples. They were familiar with prayer as an elaborate ritual of rules and with God as the Holy, Awesome Lord that only a few chosen ones would ever dare to draw near to. Did prayer have any relevance to real needs and life situations? Did God answer prayers from ordinary people or only from the powerful religious leaders? Of course, the stories of the Old Testament show that indeed God always responded to all those who genuinely called on Him. It would have been impossible for Him not to do so because God *"is the same yesterday, today and forever"* (Hebrews 13:8). The Bible shows that lives transformed, miracles of healing, provision, deliverance, signs and wonders were just as real a feature of the presence and response of God under the Old Covenant, but by the time of Jesus the personal nature of the love of God had been obscured by complex religious systems.

The secret of Jesus' powerful prayer life was expressed in that first simple phrase. To Him, prayer was connecting with God as Father. It was a connection of joy, recognising that God was a Father who could be truly honoured and worshipped. An incredible, powerful, strong, tender, loving and giving Father; a Father who wanted to protect and help His children and enable them to grow to become like Him; a Father who delighted in communicating His ways to His children and making Himself known.

HAVE YOU RECOGNISED YOUR HUNGER FOR FATHER GOD?

The disciples' hunger for reality and connection is a hunger we all feel but which often only gets acknowledged during times of stress or crisis: the big, destructive issues of family breakdown or loss – or all the moment by moment confusions and struggles of everyday life. Suddenly, in the face of such uncertainties we become aware of our hunger for God to be someone we can truly cling to. Not just a remote religious belief, or even an exciting worship experience, but a Person who we can talk to in a real way and will communicate back to us and give us personally the strength, vision and comfort we long for.

I remember going through some very difficult times as a twelve-year-old and feeling an increasing sense of desperation that there had to be "someone" out there who could help me. One day I climbed the hill supporting a bridge over a motorway. I sat for ages staring down at the frantic anonymity of the hurtling traffic. Suddenly I found myself crying and shouting "Are You there? Will You help me? Do You know what's happening to me?" I gazed up at the sky, longing for there to be an answer, something I could hold onto, but there was nothing. In the emptiness, I shouted again, "You don't exist and if You do You'll have to show me!" and flung myself down the hill, rolling at a tremendous pace towards the traffic below. I had a sense of complete abandonment. I didn't care what happened to me and there was something exhilarating about the speed and danger. I remember then the feeling of total shock when instead of smashing into the road I came to a gentle stop yards away. This made no sense as the steep gradient continued to the very edge of the motorway and there were no barriers. What had stopped me? I was afraid and lay for ages with my face pressed down in the prickly grass, feeling the pull of the slope yet aware I was doing nothing to stop myself rolling further. Eventually I dared to turn my head and open my eyes. No one was there! Yet I knew someone or something must have stopped me hitting the road. I got myself home that day and over the next few years the struggles I was facing intensified and there seemed to be no answer or help. Yet, like a seed thrusting its way up through the rocks, the awareness that something had been there to save me that afternoon, kept me going. From then on, subconsciously, I felt a deep longing to find out who or what it was.

Is God Personal and Loving?

Like me that afternoon, we ache to know if God is bigger and stronger than everything else in our lives and more than that, if He is personal and loving. Even when we have been Christians for a long time we can still find that deep in our hearts we are asking, "Is my name really known? Does who I am really count to God? Why does He seem so far away?" We often hide our questions behind our church experiences or service,

yet it's possible week by week to sing the songs, make the
responses, be excited by the sermons (hopefully!), partake of
Communion and even worship in tongues and fall on the floor
under the power of the Holy Spirit, but still not know if we are
loved by Him! We can feel embarrassed about our inner
hunger and confusion. I've often gone round thinking, "I'm a
Spirit-filled Christian attending a dynamic Spirit-filled church
and I'm in active ministry, I shouldn't be feeling this hunger."
I've felt I'm failing in some way and not living up to the
fullness of the Holy Spirit.

I am coming to see that the truth is actually the opposite!

Think of these words of wisdom that Jesus taught at the
start of the Beatitudes:

> *"Blessed are the poor in spirit,*
> *for theirs is the kingdom of heaven."*

(MATTHEW 5:3)

Jesus is saying that to be in a place of poverty of spirit is a
good thing! The word "blessed" in this context actually means,
"so happy because of God's favour that we are to be envied!"
It's when we know our own emptiness that we can ask for and
receive more and more of His presence. When He comes in,
He brings His Kingdom with Him. But in ourselves we are
poor even when in Him we are rich! We cannot say, "I was
baptised in the Spirit five years ago and I am now full of God."
Instead we can say, "I was baptised in the Spirit five years ago
and filled again this morning and will need to be filled again
tomorrow!" We can never have enough of Him, just as one
meal cannot fill us for a week or even a day. And yet always in
this life, until we meet Him face to face, there is mystery. We
can grow deeper and deeper in our understanding and
experience of Him and yet there is always something missing,
something we cannot see, something we cannot quite take
hold of except by faith, and in this is our hunger.

GLIMPSES LIKE PHOTOGRAPHS

Recently I've been taking lots of digital photographs of trees and autumn leaves. The camera is like a blank canvas waiting to capture something so beautiful or majestic. I press the button and the blankness is filled with form and colour, a beautiful picture.

And yet, when I turn from the camera to gaze back at the view, I know that what I have captured and has filled my screen is but a glimpse. It may be beautiful but it is not alive. I may see one part in the photo but not the other. And even if the colours and form of the photo are as true and clear-cut as in life, I cannot touch them or run them through my hands or climb them. The photo may indicate a hard wind is blowing, but I cannot let that wind blow on my face and sweep my hair from my eyes. It is just a glimpse. Seeing that glimpse enables me to take hold of the real to a degree, but to fully know the joy of the trees and wind and autumn leaves I need to leave the photos and go outside to be where they are. I need to let the glimpse inspire me to search for and experience the whole.

WE HAVE GLIMPSES OF GOD

In a similar way our lives are like that camera screen. Like the photos we have glimpses of God and what He is like and what He is doing. And those glimpses enter into our consciousness bringing His light, colour and beauty transforming us within and making our relationship with Him more and more real. And yet we know this is just a shadow. Every glimpse we have of Him makes us long for more and makes us more aware of our own need of Him. We want to feel that wind blowing through our hair, we are hungry to taste and smell as well as see. We want to know the full picture not just a part. God has written it within us to want more of Him. When we try to satisfy that need with other things, destruction results. But when we come to the true source and answer of our longing we are changed in the most wonderful way.

GOD OUR FATHER IS THE TRUE SOURCE AND ANSWER

But can we move from that place of being aware of our heart hunger to recognising that God as our Father will fill that hunger? What does the name Father even conjure up in our hearts? For many of us "father" evokes a feeling of dread, sadness or shame. Many of our dads have just never been there for us, either literally abandoning the family or so absorbed in themselves or their work that we can't reach them. Many of us whose dads were physically there have been crushed by their control, negativity or abusive words and actions. How then can we relate to God as Father? What does it mean? Is He going to be like what we have experienced already in our earthly dads? If He isn't like that, how will we even know? After all, we can't see Him smiling at us, or hear Him speaking words of love...

Or at least we think we can't!

The truth is that God has given us everything we need through Jesus, His Word and through the Holy Spirit to know Him as Father, and understand and experience what He is like and to hear His voice. But we do need to recognise the way our heart picture of Him may have been overwritten by the false pictures of our life experiences.

AN EXERCISE

Here is a little exercise to help you ascertain how you are approaching God as your Father. You may like to get a pen and paper and jot down any insights that come to you.

- Think again of the first line of the Lord's Prayer: "Our Father in Heaven." This indicates that He is a real person in a real location, so instead of just speaking those words into space, let's use our imaginations to make our prayer feel more real. Don't be afraid to use your imagination. It is a God-given tool for prayer.

- We all at times go and knock at the doors of people's homes and will be aware of our happy/sad, expectant/ dreading feelings towards them. So imagine now that you are walking up the front drive of "Father's house"! Jesus is with you and is taking you to visit His Dad.

- As you walk through the front garden and draw nearer to the house entrance what can you see? Is there anything about the garden or the appearance of the house that gives you a clue as to what He is like? Again, don't be afraid to use your imagination. Note down any ideas, but don't worry if nothing comes.

- Now you are standing outside the door and watching as Jesus rings the bell. How do you feel now that the moment of meeting "Father" has arrived? Note those feelings down. Don't try to be religious and put "good" things if you don't feel them. Just be honest. This is only between you and Him anyway so who is there to deceive?

- See the door open and "Father" standing there. What does He look like? What expression does He have on His face? How does He greet Jesus? How does He greet you? Note down all that comes to you.

- Now take some time to prayerfully reflect on what you have expected, experienced and written down. If your feelings as you approached that door were negative or fearful, it is probable that they are springing out of past negative experiences that need His healing touch. Similarly, if the "Father" you saw when the door was opened appeared to you as distant or dismissive or negative in any way, you are transferring those bad experiences onto your picture of

God. Simply tell Him that you seem to be seeing Him in the skin of your past experiences and ask Him to give you a new picture of the kind of Father He really is and so to free you from those old, bad pictures.

- Spend some time reflecting on these verses and asking your heavenly Father to make them real to your heart:

> *"The LORD is compassionate and gracious,*
>   *slow to anger, abounding in love."*
>
>   (PSALM 103:8)

> *"How great is the love the Father has lavished on us, that we should be called children of God! And that is what we are!"*
>
>   (1 JOHN 3:1)

WE DON'T HAVE TO SEE HIM

But is it really feasible to think we can truly connect with Someone that we cannot see or touch? Think of what Jesus said to Thomas after the resurrection:

> *"Because you have seen me, you have believed; blessed are those who have not seen me and yet have believed."*
>
>   (JOHN 20:29)

Deep down we often feel that our prayers are just words hitting the ceiling. We can easily lose all assurance that we are truly being heard by God and that He is responding to us. Yet Jesus is saying specifically here that when we choose to believe, despite the fact that we can't see Him, we will be blessed.

We need to move away from the "seeing is believing" mentality. When Thomas expressed his need to see and feel Jesus' wounds in order to believe, Jesus was not there in any visible form. And yet Jesus knew what Thomas had said and responded to it. He connected with Thomas and heard Thomas' words and understood his need. Thomas probably did not think that he was praying when he expressed his doubts to his friends. He certainly did not realize that Jesus was there listening to him! But Jesus *was* there, just in a different way to what Thomas was used to. And as He later lovingly responded to all Thomas had said, Thomas could only declare in astonishment, *"My Lord and my God."*

If we think about it, much of our present-day communication is through non-visual means. We are so used to the idea of making contact with colleagues and loved ones through telephones, texting and computers that we don't even think about it. Yet it is actually mind boggling to think we can stand in our own home, press a few buttons on a gadget and suddenly be connected with someone hundreds or thousands of miles away. We may say, "That is different because I hear their voice or I see their words come up on my screen" but in reality we have no tangible proof that it is really them. The voice may sound like them and we accept it is them because we are used to the concept of connecting to them in this way, but really we are connecting to them through faith in a gadget! Can we therefore not trust that we really are connecting to God through our prayers?

A Personal Illustration

Not so long ago I was returning home by train late in the evening after attending a wedding. I knew Marilyn had ordered a taxi for me from Vernon, a driver who knows us well and always takes care to ensure we are okay. (I am partially sighted as well as deaf.)

When I arrived at the station I very confidently marched into the entrance fully expecting to see Vernon waiting and was shocked to find he wasn't there. I went to wait outside and was even more shocked when I discovered a huge, rowdy crowd, ambulances and police cars. People were drunk, there were bottles flying through the air and some people were fighting. I looked frantically for Vernon but he was nowhere to be seen! I couldn't believe it as he always came right into the foyer to meet us. I couldn't ring Marilyn and the fight was all round the taxi rank so I couldn't imagine how to get home. I felt very panicky. By now it was nearly midnight and I knew I was in a vulnerable position. So I prayed very simply, "Father, please come and look after me, please give me Your peace and help me to get home safely."

Amazingly the anxiety lifted and I knew I would be okay, even though the disturbance was getting more serious. About ten minutes went by and I hadn't seen anyone else coming out of the station. But suddenly I felt a tap on my shoulder and when I turned round there was a lady from my church! She asked me if I had a lift and when I told her I was stuck she said Paul, her husband, would take me home too. I was amazed. In all the years and thousands of times I'd used that station I'd never met anyone I knew and this was so late at night. But I know that God my Father was bringing it all together in an incredible way. He heard my fear and knew my need. He responded to my simple prayer. He gave me His peace and had all the practical timings taken care of to get me safely home.

(I later discovered that Vernon had come for me but his car had been damaged by the mob and he'd had to go to the Police, and then could not get back to me as his car was off the road.)

A PRAYER

Lord, I want so much to know You. I am hungry, Father. I long for reality and for that hole inside me to be filled with You. I long to connect with You as Jesus did. Thank You that You heard and answered Thomas' deepest need, even when You weren't there physically. Thank You that You hear and meet my deepest needs too. You alone can satisfy me. You are "the air I breathe". You are my "daily bread". Thank You, dear Father, that You give me all I need. Amen.

Note

1. Marie Barnett, 1995, © Mercy/Vineyard Publishing/Copycare.

CHAPTER 2

THE SKELETON KEY OF TRUST

"Trust in the LORD with all your heart
and lean not on your own understanding;
in all your ways acknowledge him,
and he will make your paths straight."
(PROVERBS 3:5–6)

When I was about ten I remember being given a mock skeleton key for Christmas. I was fascinated with the concept of being able to open any door I wanted with this key. Of course, in reality my key was useless as it was just a cheap toy, but that didn't stop me acting out my imaginings! It was very exciting to think that with this key I was more powerful than any lock. No door could withstand me when I had my key!

Locked Doors

In real life, we constantly come up against doors that seem so securely locked that we feel we will never get through them. Sometimes these are external doors created by governments and culture, or the judgements and rejections of others. Often they are internal doors like the inward drives that control us, our fears or inadequacies, our feelings of worthlessness, shame or anger, our illnesses or disabilities ... We long to break free but the doors are locked. We cannot imagine ever seeing beyond them, let alone going through them.

But God has given us the keys to life's locked doors and one in particular that just like a skeleton key gives access to all the doors, is called *Trust*.

What is Trust?

What is trust? How can we describe it? At its highest it is a heart knowing, not just that God is there but that He is *good*. Not just that He is good, but that He is good *to me*. Not just that He is the Creator and His nature is Love, but that He lovingly created *me*. Not just that He speaks, but that He speaks *to me*. Not just that He is strong and powerful, but that He comes in His strength and power to *strengthen me*. That He is *my* Saviour, *my* Father and friend, *my* Shepherd; or, as Paul puts it more succinctly in Romans:

> *"If God is for us, who can be against us? He who did not spare his own Son, but gave him up for us all – how will he not also, along with him, graciously give us all things?"*
>
> (Romans 8:31)

Paul was not naïve. He knew that life is not one big party. He was going through rejection, poverty, hunger, betrayal and abuse even as he wrote these words. And yet he had a knowing in his heart, that went deeper than every other element of his life, that God loved him and was actively working for his good. And Paul had chosen to jump off the cliff edge of doubt and entrust himself radically to that love.

This kind of trust is rare indeed in our wary, postmodern society. The very nature of postmodernism is that there are no boundaries. Everything is questionable. Every political move is debated from all angles in the media and everyone decides their own answer. There are no more good or bad values, but human rights and political correctness form the modern bible. We are saddened but not shocked to hear of corrupt police or economists, or that a hospital leaves a ninety-one-year-old patient to starve, that a sex offender is released in weeks while a man defending himself against assault serves fifteen years, or that a husband has an affair while his wife is pregnant with their first child...

In this cultural framework, trust of any form, whether in God or man or simply in the existence of goodness and beauty, is interpreted as naivety, and it's not cool to be naïve!

But Paul has a clear cut answer:

"Do not conform any longer to the pattern of this world, but be transformed by the renewing of your mind. Then you will be able to test and approve what God's will is – his good, pleasing and perfect will."
(ROMANS 12:2)

AS WE TRUST GOD HE TRANSFORMS US

God is in the business of transforming us. Where life and our own choices have wounded our spirits and made us wary and cautious of every step, He comes to us as loving Father and says, "Child, I love you with an everlasting love, trust Me. I will never ever leave you, trust Me. You are the apple of My eye, trust Me. I forgive your every sin, heal your every wound and provide for your every need, trust Me. I give you a hope and a future, trust Me. I choose you to be My friend and My bride, you are beautiful without any flaw to Me, trust Me..."[1]

But how can we respond to God's words and promises? How can we enter into this transforming process? The key is what we allow our minds to be filled with and to focus on. It is all too easy, when painful things happen, to let our wounds dictate our thinking. We can spend hours mentally going over and over what happened but then find ourselves locked into a prison of pain. Or we can listen to God and choose to focus on His love, and as we make that choice, often while still in the throes of our pain or fear, God comes to us and touches us with His love, and transforms us inside, giving us His peace, healing and enabling.

A Personal Illustration

In my work with Marilyn I am in a very "up-front" position, but the years of being thought stupid at school, before my deafness was properly diagnosed, gave me a deep fear of being on public view. The fact that my co-ordination is poor and I am often jerky in my movements also enhances this self-consciousness. Often as I sit in a concert waiting to speak I am aware of these old feelings of shame and I panic, feeling certain that I am going to let God down and look a complete fool. But in my heart I start to feel a nudging, a kind of awareness that God is longing to reach out to people with His love and bathe their lives with hope and peace. It's as if He is saying to me, "If you trust Me to flow through you to touch people then that is what they will see and hear. They won't be thinking 'what an idiot.'" And amazingly time and again I have seen that happen. That as I've made the choice to trust Him to give me all I need, my fearful heart has melted and I've found myself passionately wanting people to know His love. Instead of dreading people seeing me, I just want to communicate how incredible He is. I forget how panicky I was a moment before. I become glad and full of amazement that He is using *me* to communicate what He is like.

Sometimes people tell me, "What you said was so powerful, you radiated the love of God . . . " And I feel stunned because in my mind I've been all too aware of my awkwardness and muddles. Yet God has worked despite that, or maybe even within that.

Trust Means Stepping Out of Our Fear Zones

Trust is both a heart decision and an action.

One may have thought that with the Lord being so full of understanding and compassionate love, He would never ask us to do things that rock the painful areas of our lives. But He loves us far too much to let us stay in those prisons! I have often found that it is in the very act of listening to His heart for people, then speaking out in public what He gives me, that opens the door of healing in my own memories. Because I am afraid, I know I have to trust Him. Then, incredibly, I find I come alive and feel a deep inner joy in areas of my life that have previously been full of shame. But if I stay in a cocoon, safely cloistered where no one can see me, I am giving those old fears more and more power to control me.

Marilyn has a guide dog called Pennie. As well as serious work to get Marilyn to important places, Pennie also frequently visits the field for a free run. I walk behind so as not to distract Pennie from her work. As I watch them both, I am always amazed at how this little walk creates such an incredible picture of what trust is meant to be.

With no sight, Marilyn has to rely completely on Pennie to get her safely round any obstacles. Although the field is just round the corner, she has to navigate her way through a zigzag gate at the entrance of a narrow footpath, itself often strewn with bicycles and bounded at the far end with concrete pillars.

Then she has to go past several large dustbins, turn into the main gate of the field and immediately round another two gates before she is there!

Pennie knows full well that this walk will end in her favourite treat, the free run. She adores running and takes off like a greyhound as soon as she is released! Yet despite that enthusiasm, she never fails to do her best to get Marilyn safely round all the obstacles. Of course, she is only a dog and sometimes she does make mistakes, *but,* Marilyn still trusts her.

If Marilyn did not trust Pennie, Pennie would not be able to guide her. Just imagine it, the blind person pulling back and panicking at every step in case she trips or hits something in her path. The dog would become frightened and confused and would refuse to work. But Marilyn makes a choice that she will trust Pennie. Sometimes she does feel nervous, especially if Pennie has bumped her into something on a previous walk, but she still makes that choice to trust and follow. She relaxes her body so that she can feel Pennie through the harness handle and then follows every move that Pennie makes. A step to the right, an immediate left, a sharp right and forward and she's through the cycle gate without touching a single rail and so on round the pillars, bicycles and bins!

What Am I Getting At?

With all this talk about Pennie, what am I getting at? Well, the fact that Marilyn can see neither the way ahead, nor the dog she is trusting to lead her safely, is a wonderful picture of what our trust in God is meant to be like. We often cannot see the way ahead in life or how to deal with a situation, nor can we see our God, who is the only One who can effectively lead us. So, just as Marilyn has to choose to trust Pennie, even when she feels nervous, so we need to choose to trust God. Deciding to trust means an actual act of stepping out in some way. If Marilyn were to just wave the guide dog harness around in the air, or even put it on Pennie, but not go out alone with her, then she would just be displaying the symbols of having a guide dog. Similarly, if we just carry our Bibles around, talk about praying and even have a quiet time and time to pray, but have no heart trust then we are just displaying the symbols of being a Christian!

We Don't Have to See Everything in Order to Trust

Marilyn makes a choice to trust her dog with her safety. The fact that she cannot see where she is going, nor see Pennie, does not strip her of the power to trust. We often presume that in order to trust we have to understand, and in order to understand we have to experience with our senses. Yet although all these things help, our power to trust does not have to depend on them. We have to decide to trust just as Marilyn has to choose to trust Pennie. It is a decision we make irrespective of what the circumstances may be.

The *Oxford Thesaurus* gives the following word alternatives to "trust": "faith; confidence; belief; conviction; credence; assurance; certainty: reliance; hope; expectation ... "[2]

Just reading these words engenders a feeling of *"Yes!"* in me. They are all intrinsic, coming from a deep place of knowing and rest. They are all "good" words. When you trust you are expecting something good to happen! It's not possible to trust for something bad. We may *expect* something bad to happen but that is not trust, it is dread!

When we've loved someone only to have them betray us, or trusted someone only to have them take advantage of us, a little more of our natural trust is stripped away each time, leaving the soul-deadening inevitability of things always going wrong. We hear words about the love and power of Jesus with a wistful yet cynical, "Well it may happen for some but not for me!" This cynicism is coming out of a place of hurt and fear.

We have been let down before and now are too afraid to expose ourselves to that hurt again. But John wrote:

> *"There is no fear in love. But perfect love drives out fear, because fear has to do with punishment."*

(1 JOHN 4:18)

This is the answer to our broken ability to trust. John tells us the wonderfully healing truth that this love from Jesus has the power to drive our fears away. He is not there to punish but instead He is the healer of our bad experiences and resulting cynicism. God offers us perfect love. As we take hold of it, meditate on it, talk to Him and let Him talk back to us and take the steps that He puts on our hearts to take, out of that perfect love we discover the gift of being able to trust coming alive again.

I Can't Trust until I Feel Trusting

As a deaf person I have a constant struggle to know and be part of what's going on. The merrier a social situation, the more miserable I am tempted to feel! I can very easily go into self-pity mode: "I'm so boring, I'm always on the outside, I always say the wrong thing..." (There will be an example of how God challenged me when I was in this mode in the next chapter!)

But if I feel floored by things like that, how much more does someone feel when they learn that their husband of thirty years is having an affair with another woman? How do we respond when we discover our child has suffered abuse or when we have to face allegations of misconduct that will permanently scar our credibility? How do we cope when we are struggling with a disability and then hear that our partner or child has become seriously ill and needs constant care? Not forgetting the scars from the past that constantly cripple the present. Memories of childhood abuse, rejection, shame, abandonment and loss, to name just a few.

All of these life situations are wearyingly destructive and make us feel as if we are under a black cloud and there is no way out. We use so much energy struggling just to live under the weight of it all that it seems impossible to think of God or to pray with any real hope that He really cares, let alone will answer and work on our behalf to help us. Yet this is the very thing God most longs to do. We may say with perfect logic, "Well, I will trust in God once I've seen that His love is real and seen how He has resolved my situation" but in fact it is our very trust that both enables us to see clearly and provides the key for God to step into those situations! Trust is the act of clinging on in terror! In ourselves we may fall, but trust is the grabbing hold of the strong, steady arm and walking with its support along the edge of the abyss.

A PERSONAL ILLUSTRATION

Recently while staying at Loyola Hall (the retreat centre referred to in the Introduction), I came under extreme attack from old fears. As I returned to my room one evening I had to pass a queue of men along the corridor. They were on a different retreat and I did not know them but knew they were all Christians. I was surprised therefore to find myself feeling vulnerable as I walked past them but prayed and tried to dismiss the feelings. My room was at the end of the corridor with the stairwell just beyond it. As I went to unlock my door I glanced casually into the stairwell area and froze. There was a man there in the shadows, standing completely motionless, staring at me. I was suddenly terrified. I managed to unlock the door and fell into my room hardly able to breathe. I didn't know what to do. I couldn't think or pray. Deep down I knew it was completely irrational – this was a Christian centre and the man was just one of the queue waiting to speak to his spiritual director. But as much as I knew that, it couldn't shake the fear and the "certainty" of what was going to happen next. Marilyn often quotes an acronym to describe this kind of counterfeit certainty:

False
Evidence
Appearing
Real

This was certainly the case here. Fear from past experiences was paralysing me and whatever logic I thought of or prayers I prayed, nothing helped. I could neither stay in the room nor leave. My jaw locked, I was breathing in gasps and shaking. I tried to resist the devil and claim the name of Jesus, all to no avail. I remember half thinking, half praying, "God, if You are really here, take this fear away!"

And He answered me. He said, "Go out of this room with Me at your side. Go past the men and down to the kitchen with Me at your side. Make yourself a hot drink and then come back again still with Me at your side."

He had not taken my fear away. He had not soothed and patted me better. Nor had He told me I was silly or sinful to be afraid and needed to have more faith. *Instead He showed me the way of trust.*

It may sound melodramatic to someone who has never been gripped by such fears. But it is the simple truth that it was one of the hardest things I have ever done to walk out of that room again and back past those men. All the way down the corridor I was muttering under my breath, "You're with me, You're with me. Help me, help me." I asked Him to come into the kitchen with me and stand between me and the door. I managed to make the drink and then had to face the corridor again. The fear still gripped me. Again, I asked Him to be with me and help me each step back and, incredibly, made it to the room without spilling a drop. Those of you who know about my poor balance will know what a miracle that was! The hot drink helped me. I started to breathe more naturally and the heat relaxed my jaws. But I was still too afraid to stay in my room. I felt I needed help, so once I finished the drink I went out, again affirming over and over that He was with me. I prayed He would help me find my spiritual director (a lady) or another female member of the community, but I only met more male retreatants!

I knew He wanted me to go back to my room and trust Him alone to protect me there. After all, how could anyone really help? As loving or wise as they might be they couldn't take the fear from me. Only God could do that. I wished He had taken it away when it first hit me! But He just seemed to be calling me to face it together with Him.

I did go back to my room and for a long while still felt extremely anxious. Many of our fears, even when irrational, hinge on past traumas and that was certainly the case in this experience. So it wasn't simply that I needed releasing from a satanic attack but that the child part of me, the part that had been betrayed and wounded, needed healing and her trust restoring. Throughout the rest of that evening I sensed Him with me, suggesting I do practical things like putting my photographs onto the computer, which proved a lovely exercise, tidying my room, writing up my journal. It was as if He was there as loving Father with His frightened child, wisely helping her create a true picture of love, order and beauty and see His part in all of that.

When I went to bed I asked Him to stay with me and watch over me. I was still fearful but deliberately chose to affirm aloud that I would trust Him to look after me. Then I went to sleep! Amazingly, I slept through the whole night and when I woke the next morning I knew the fear had gone. There was a lightness and a warmth inside me, as if something had come back to life that had been dead for a very long time.

I have not had another such fear since.

A Prayer Exercise

Read again through this paragraph containing just some of God's love promises to you and affirmations of how He sees you:

> *"Child, I love you with an everlasting love, trust Me. I will never ever leave you, trust Me. You are the apple of My eye, trust Me. I forgive your every sin, heal your every wound and provide for your every need, trust Me. I give you a hope and a future, trust Me. I choose you to be My friend and My bride, you are beautiful without any flaw to Me, trust Me...*"[3]

- Take time to reflect. Even if you can't feel the truth of these words, do you want to believe them? Do you want these and all of God's promises to you to be the foundations of your life and faith?
- If the answer is yes, ask the Holy Spirit to make the prayer below real to you and to start to heal the broken areas of trust in your life.
- Now pray these words back to Him, making it personal and changing His request to "trust Me" to your response, "Father, I will trust You."

"Father, I trust that You love me with an everlasting love. Father, I trust that You will never, ever leave me. Father, I trust that I am the apple of Your eye. Father, I trust that You forgive my every sin, heal my every wound and provide for my every need. Father, I trust that You give me a hope and a future. Father, I trust that You choose me to be Your friend and bride, that I am beautiful without any flaw to You, and, Father, I choose to trust that You are good in every way and will fulfil all Your promises to me, In Jesus' wonderful name. Amen."[4]

Notes

1. See Jeremiah 31:3; Hebrews 13:5b; Deuteronomy 32:10b; Psalm 103:3; Isaiah 53:5; Philippians 4:19; Jeremiah 29:11; John 15:15; Revelation 19:7; Song of Solomon 4:7.
2. *The Oxford Large Print Thesaurus*, Oxford University Press, 1997.
3. See Jeremiah 31:3; Hebrews 13:5b; Deuteronomy 32:10b; Psalm 103:3; Isaiah 53:5; Philippians 4:19; Jeremiah 29:11; John 15:15; Revelation 19:7; Song of Solomon 4:7.
4. See Jeremiah 31:3; Hebrews 13:5b; Deuteronomy 32:10b; Psalm 103:3; Isaiah 53:5; Philippians 4:19; Jeremiah 29:11; John 15:15; Revelation 19:7; Song of Solomon 4:7.

CHAPTER 3

THE TAP ON
THE SHOULDER

*"While they were still talking ... Jesus himself stood among them
and said to them, 'Peace be with you.' They were startled ...
And while they still did not believe it because of joy and
amazement, he asked them, 'Do you have anything here to eat?' "*
(LUKE 24:36–47, 41)

I was going to spend a few days with my sister. When I arrived
she said to me, "I'm going out tonight for a Chinese meal with
some friends. Would you like to come?"

Well, I was always up for a good meal and Chinese is one of
my favourites, so I said "Yes".

The food was lovely but for me there was a problem. I
could not hear any of the conversations. Here I was in the
midst of this group, most of whom I'd never met before, talk

41

and laughter rioting all round me, but with no idea what was going on! I couldn't dig out a notebook and ask people to write down what they were saying, everything was moving much too fast for that! Nor could I think, "Oh well, it won't go on like this for long." I knew they would be at it for several hours yet! So I tried to pretend that I was part of it all, looking at each person as they talked, laughing when everyone laughed, but I began to feel so small. "All these ladies look so together," I thought miserably. "I just can't match up to them; I am so hopeless at social things." I ducked my head, stared at my plate and went into self-pity mode!

After about an hour of this, God spoke to me. He put a clear question in my mind. It startled me, because by then I'd got myself so entrenched in my negative thoughts. He asked, *"Tracy, why are you spending all this time just staring at your plate?"*

"Because I'm not part of this group and don't know how to be!"

"Why not?"

"Lord, You know why! I can't hear anything that's happening! I can't laugh at the funny stories! These ladies are all so sociable and I feel inferior and a real failure socially."

"But how can you feel inferior when you are the daughter of a King?"

I stopped in my tracks. This thought had come into my consciousness with such clarity that I knew for sure it must be God. It was the kind of thing I had often said myself when trying to encourage people with low self-esteem, yet I obviously had not believed it enough for myself!

"Don't you realize I am here with you?" He continued. *"You are not on your own in this group, I am by your side. I want to talk with you and enjoy this meal with you. I want to share My thoughts and give you My heart to pray for these ladies. They are not as 'together' as you think. Lift up your head and look at them with My eyes of love. Be the beautiful daughter I've made you to be."*

I was so amazed at these words that I immediately told Him

I was sorry for being self-pitying and asked Him to forgive me and give me a new perspective. I did look up again. The conversations and laughter were still buzzing all round me, but I felt different. I had an incredible sense that Jesus was truly sitting next to me, a glorious secret between Him and me. As the meal progressed He kept speaking into my heart of His love for these ladies. It was as if I was seeing beyond their smart exteriors to their inner pain and struggles. *"You may not be able to hear them,"* He said, *"but you can hear Me and know My love. The real tragedy is that none of these know how much I love them and want to help them."*

I found myself praying with a heart longing that they would all find God's love for themselves. A window seemed to open into the group and suddenly I was laughing naturally with them and chipped in on a couple of occasions with some funny stories of my own. Most of the time I still remained silent, but it was such a different silence. Gone was the deep feeling of inferiority. Instead I was a secret princess with my King at my side, enjoying conversing with Him and the enabling He gave me to be part of that group, even though I still couldn't hear a word! At the end of that time I left with my head held high and so full of gratitude at the way He had come to me and lovingly changed my perspective.

God Takes the Initiative

In that restaurant God took the initiative to break into my thoughts. I wasn't praying or seeking His face. Even though I was struggling, I had not thought to ask Him for help, but was just getting more and more stuck in my miserable thoughts.

But God didn't let me stay there!

One of the most amazing aspects of our relationship with God is that as Father and friend He comes to us and, as it were, taps on our shoulder to get our attention. With Marilyn's blindness, she is not always aware I am there, especially if

she is absorbed in something, so I may tap her on the shoulder
to get her attention. Similarly we are not always aware that
God is with us, but He does not want to just be a silent
witness at our side. He wants to connect and to speak with us
and for us to speak with Him. He made us for friendship with
Him and will do everything to open up communication
between us. He rejoices when we choose to pray and come
to Him for help with our needs and struggles. But He also
loves to come to us unexpectedly, to break into our everyday, to take the humdrum moment and make it rich and
dynamic by entering it in such a way that it becomes holy.
Listen to these moving words from Hosea 11 where God
expresses through the prophet the way He has tried repeatedly
to reach His people through human means and His heartbreak
when we have turned away from Him and not recognised
Him.

> *"When Israel was a child I loved him as a son and I called my son
> out of Egypt ... But the more I called him the more he rebelled ...
> It was I who taught Israel to walk, leading him along by the hand.
> But he doesn't know or even care that it was I who took care of
> him. I led him along with my ropes of kindness and love. I lifted the
> yoke from his neck and myself stooped to feed him."*
>
> (HOSEA 11:1–4 précis, NLT)

Every time I read this passage I feel the deep longing of Father
God to be close to us. To Him the nation Israel was never just
a mass of humanity but a precious son. And in the same way,
we are never just His church or His body, but the ones for
whom He has given everything to make us His beloved sons
and daughters. He called Israel out of the place of slavery and
led them through the desert to become royal heirs and princes.
Through the death of Jesus He also frees us from slavery to
the many things of life we try to find fulfilment in and draws
us instead into relationship with Him on an everyday basis.

Think of the tenderness of the picture this Hosea prophecy paints for us: the loving, "hands on" Dad, feeding His children, teaching them to walk, holding them by the hand, guiding and protecting them, longing for them to turn their heads and recognise Him.

Some may feel that this is just a picture – beautiful but abstract and God seems to be just "out there" somewhere. Sometimes we may sense Him in church or in the Bible or a hymn, but not in the place where we itch – the emptiness of loss, the lack of fulfilling work or the cut and thrust of our busy daily lives.

But it is my belief and experience that this picture of God as a caring, tender-hearted and present Father is far more than a beautiful idea. God is showing in this passage that the ordinary things of life are a means for Him to draw close to us and speak to us, as His cared for child. He is in the midst of those activities that are essential to life yet taken for granted. He wants to use our everyday lives to give us sudden illuminations of His character and new insights into what He is saying to us.

A FRIEND'S STORY

Chris, a friend I made recently at a retreat, wrote to share her story of how she tried to bond with her new granddaughter who was born with severe mental and physical disabilities, and the understanding this gave her of God's love for us. In her own words:

"It was impossible to get to know this child in the same way as an ordinary baby. Whenever we used to visit her I would spend ages just lying alongside her, just spending time with her, just the two of us together; having no expectations of her – just being there together. And although she might not look at me or show any signs of knowing I was there, somehow I came to feel there was some communication going on between us. Somehow I knew I was getting to 'know' her. And I came to feel that she was wanting to get to know me. It was all just totally beautiful. And then I realized that this was really how we get to know God; to just be together and to enjoy that 'being' together. God was wanting to communicate and to be there and that as we spend time with Him we realize we are coming to know Him ...

The love I give Hazel has to be unconditional. There are no guarantees of anything coming back. She is likely to turn away from me and show no interest in me, to ignore me. She may seem totally involved and happy in her world and not want to 'come in' to mine. She may be irritable ... and yet I love this child. I stay alongside her and my love grows, so that if she does show signs of knowing I am there, if she does turn towards me and seems curious about me, if she does seem happy to be near me and to be wanting to be with me, then my whole world explodes with such joy. If she is not doing well, not developing, ill, in pain, then I suffer, I feel sorrow. All I want is for her to know I am there, that I love her, that she is surrounded by love.

And then this made me understand more clearly the unconditional love God gives us. Even if we turn away from Him and show no interest in Him, even if we totally ignore Him because we are so busy in our own lives, His love still surrounds us and is within us. There are no conditions. And I was shown that when we do reach out to Him, when we do get curious about Him and turn to Him, He feels absolute joy. He really does feel joy. I saw that He feels pain when we feel pain. He is happy when we are happy. He just wants us to know He is there. He just wants to surround us with love and for us to know we are loved."[1]

I was so humbled when I read this. When I met Chris I could tell how deeply she loved Hazel. Her love shone out of her and sounded in her words. Yet this was love birthed in pain. She had been through the fire of realizing that her longed for grandchild was so disabled. There had been the anguish of "*Why?*", the ongoing concern for her daughter and the burden she has to carry, and the grief of knowing that normal children's milestones will never be Hazel's. And yet, where so many would become bitter, or at least doubt the love of God, Chris has allowed Him to transform her pain, to let the very process of loving this child become a picture of how He loves us, and to receive His insight that Hazel's life is actually a gift to teach many about love and that having her would help Chris herself to be compassionate. I have seen this deep compassion flowing through Chris and it makes me realize the wonderful fruit of allowing God to come into our situations, to speak to us through them and transform our perceptions.

THE TREASURE IN THE FIELD

Jesus told an amazing parable about the kingdom of heaven:

> *"The kingdom of heaven is like treasure hidden in a field. When a man found it, he hid it again, and then in his joy went and sold all he had and bought that field."*
>
> (MATTHEW 13:44)

There is nothing more dynamic than the kingdom of heaven and nothing more ordinary than a field! Jesus was passionate to introduce us to the Father who loves to play with us. Do we expect to suddenly get a glimpse of something beautiful in the midst of our daily routine? He calls to us from the field, the office, the nursery, the kitchen: "Hey, can you see Me?" And that moment of encounter is exuberantly rich and life changing. We often portray God as being serious and formal, a

stickler for rules. Yet He shows Himself as so different –
playful, fun-loving, wanting us to experience joy and to be able
to throw caution to the wind because He has given us something greater to aim for. I often wonder how Simon Peter and
Andrew felt while, when hard at work fishing and mending
nets, they heard those incredible words:

> *"Come, follow me ... and I will make you fishers of men."*
> (MATTHEW 4:19)

It was as if in that moment a door opened into the ordinary,
routine nature of their lives. There was an immediate sense of
identification, yet they knew He wasn't just chatting about
fishing. He was using the familiar to speak into their inner lives
in a riveting and life-changing way. They saw a glimpse of an
exciting new dimension to living, one that was so enthralling
they chose to leave everything to follow Him.

HE SPEAKS THROUGH ORDINARY THINGS, BUT TO EXTRAORDINARY EFFECT

Jesus' words are like treasure because they are full of power.
He never speaks just for the sake of filling the silence, as we so
often do. Instead His words are pithy and uncompromisingly
real, yet so full of tender love that they melt us inside.

When I was on the retreat referred to earlier, I was feeling
low one day. I sat in the various quiet rooms and chapels,
trying to pray, but as time went by the more empty I felt.
Finally I gave up and went to the little guest kitchen to make a
cup of tea. I had grown fond of a certain mug that was
decorated with autumn leaves. I reached for it but it wasn't on
the shelf. Someone else must have taken it. I was a bit fed up.
Not having "my" mug seemed like the last straw after a
fruitless day. I made my tea in another mug and after a couple
of sips headed for the door. While changing the mug to my left

hand, I suddenly realized that it was, after all, "my" mug! It had been on a different shelf and I just hadn't recognised it. I was pleased and in that moment of happy discovery, God suddenly spoke to me:

"You felt you had lost that mug but you were actually holding it and drinking from it. In the same way you feel you have lost Me today but you have been holding Me and I have been holding you and you have been drinking from Me, even when you haven't realized it was Me!"

I can still remember now the awe that filled me in the kitchen as I stood there clutching "my" mug! I hadn't been able to find Him in all the specifically spiritual places, but He had been with me all the time and had chosen to make Himself known through something as ordinary as a mug of tea! Unlike the fleeting effects of human words, I was transfixed and changed by this "meeting" with my heavenly Father. It revealed to me afresh how intimately He knew me and was aware of the most mundane details of my habits. As these verses from Psalm 139 express:

"You know when I sit down or stand up.
*   You know my thoughts even when I'm far away.*
You see me when I travel
*   and when I rest at home.*
*   You know everything I do.*
You know what I am going to say
*   even before I say it, LORD."*

(PSALM 139:2–4, NLT)

GOD WANTS US TO KNOW HIS JOY

Jesus told His disciples:

"I have loved you even as the Father has loved me. Remain in my love ... I have told you these things so that you will be filled with my joy. Yes, your joy will overflow!"

(JOHN 15:9, 11 NLT)

"I have told you this so that my joy may be in you and that your joy may be complete."

(JOHN 15:11)

As I look back on that experience in the kitchen I can still feel the intense joy that filled me in that moment. As Christians we know that joy and peace are two of our great salvation promises, but many feel they always have to be happy, and it seems blasphemy to admit to sadness, struggle or doubt. This often results in a false, frothy, "happy-clappy" kind of "front", but hidden behind it is sadness over many things which, if never acknowledged, can ultimately destroy our faith. Yet, we only need to look honestly at the life of Jesus to realize that while He was the most joy-filled person there has ever been, He also freely experienced and expressed deep emotions including the "baddies" of grief, despair, anger and fear!

Knowing the joy of the Lord is nothing to do with denying all our negative emotions but everything to do with the ongoing awareness that in His love He is there with us, and that somehow through that very fact of His presence, the power of His love gives us comfort and strength and new vision.

He takes the dust of our lives and turns it into diamonds.

The other day I was doing some household chores and was very conscious of all the things that needed doing and the little time I had to do them in. I was feeling somewhat stressed and panicky when suddenly a thought jumped into my mind about how amazing it was that Jesus was with me and was facing each task with me. Such a simple thought but I was suddenly suffused with a feeling of intense joy. Knowing He was with me in such an intimate way (after all what could be more intimate than choosing to be alongside someone as they clean the bathroom and change beds?), gave me a deep sense of His friendship and love. It completely changed the colour of the day from a monotonous grey to a golden yellow. Like Andrew and Simon Peter, God had come to me and spoken to me very simply through my chores. The effect was incredible. I can still feel the joy now as I write!

The words we hear from Jesus and the ways He enables us to experience Him, are what bring us joy and as that verse from John 15 expresses, it is a *complete* joy. That doesn't mean we will always be up on cloud nine; we may be acting quite soberly, yet inside us there will be a bubble that lifts us up and excites us and compels us to talk with Him and listen more for the things He wants to say to us.

AN EXERCISE

Get on with doing some task or chore you need to do. Take note of any feelings you have e.g. boredom, anxiety, irritation.

- Think of these words from Psalm 139:

> *"O LORD, you have searched me*
> *and you know me.*
> *You know when I sit and when I rise;*
> *you perceive my thoughts from afar.*
> *You discern my going out and my lying down;*
> *you are familiar with all my ways.*
> *Before a word is on my tongue*
> *you know it completely, O LORD."*
>
> (PSALM 139:1–4)

- Allow one of those phrases to stay in your mind. *"You know me."* Mull over that phrase as you continue to get on with your job. Thank Him that knowing you like that can only mean He is with you right at that moment and wanting to be involved in what you are doing and feeling.
- Tell Him how you are feeling and then say to Him very simply, "Is there anything You want to say to me, Lord?

Any way You want to make me more aware of Your presence?" Allow the thing you are doing in itself to become a means of Him touching you. For example, if you are bathing your children for bed, let your thoughts turn to His tender care for you. If you are working in business, focus on His incredible eye for detail; if you are cleaning or ironing thank Him for the wonderful and complete way He brings cleansing into your life and covers you with His perfection...

- As you allow the job at hand to become a means of worship and thanksgiving, give time for listening to what He might want to say specifically to you, just as He did to Simon and Andrew through their fishing. Take note of any thoughts that come into your mind, don't just dismiss them as imagination. It is through our imaginations that He reaches us!

- Allow any idea or thought that has come to you to take root in your heart. Think about it. Thank Him for it and for His love in drawing close to you. Ask Him to help you make it real in your life. If you keep a journal, record there what God has said to you.

Note

1. Christine Bromley. Quoted and paraphrased from a personal letter and used by permission .

CHAPTER 4

LIFE-CHANGING DIALOGUE

"God called to him from within the bush, 'Moses! Moses!'
And Moses said, 'Here I am.'"
(EXODUS 3:4)

THE THRILL OF GOD CALLING TO US

The above verse is one example of some of the most exciting phrases in the Bible: "The word of the Lord came to ... God called to ... God came to ... in a vision..." etc.

Whenever I read such words I feel a tremendous thrill. It's as if God is emphasizing:

*"**I** am the God who speaks and draws you into communion with Me.*

I come to where you are and make Myself known to you.
I call your name and listen for your response.
I daily reveal My heart of love to you and open up My longings
that you may be part of all I am doing."

Jesus, who said He could only do what He saw His heavenly Father doing, spoke to all who would listen in language that was far easier to understand than the elaborate language used by the religious leaders. He engaged in conversation with those who were in need and listened to their responses. He spoke to people by name and affirmed them. He answered people's questions and challenged their ungodly blind spots. He reached out to people who had no expectation of Him talking to *them* and with divinely inspired knowledge ministered healing and release.

Jesus was empowered to hear God and powerfully communicate God's heart by the Holy Spirit who came upon Him in the form of a dove at Jesus' baptism and whose first work was to enable Jesus Himself to hear the Father's affirmation: *"This is my Son, whom I love; with him I am well pleased"* (Matthew 3:17).

Jesus told us that we too would receive the same Spirit who would communicate to us as He had to Jesus; we would be empowered to know what God is doing and brought into partnership with His purposes:

"The Counsellor, the Holy Spirit whom the Father will send in my name, will teach you all things and will remind you of everything I have said to you ... The Spirit of Truth lives with you and will be in you. I will not leave you as orphans, I will come to you ... I will send the Counsellor to you ... He will convict the world of guilt in regard to sin and righteousness and judgement ... He will guide you into all truth. He will not speak on his own; he will speak only what he hears, and he will tell you what is yet to come. He will bring glory to me by taking from what is mine and making it known to you."

(JOHN 14:26, 17–18; 16:7–8, 13–14 précis)

Following the ascension Jesus' promise was fulfilled when the disciples were filled with the Holy Spirit on the day of Pentecost. It is tremendously significant to see that it was *after* this, rather than before when they were physically with Jesus, that they came into a whole new dimension of revelation, power, effectiveness in ministry and most importantly, love and compassion instead of self-absorption.

So How Do We Live in This New Dimension?

Isaiah expressed a powerful key to communicating with God:

> *"The Sovereign LORD has given me an instructed tongue,*
> *to know the word that sustains the weary.*
> *He wakens me morning by morning,*
> *wakens my ear to listen like one being taught.*
> *The Sovereign LORD has opened my ears,*
> *and I have not been rebellious;*
> *I have not drawn back."*

(ISAIAH 50:4–5)

God is the one who "wakens" our ears and enables us to "hear" His voice. Our responsibility is to listen. This listening is not primarily with our physical ears but with our spirit.

The Holy Spirit empowers us but, as Isaiah expresses here, we need to become *"like one being taught"*. It takes practice to learn to recognise His voice and respond to Him, but Isaiah brought alive the fact that God is with us constantly. He wakens us and then is with us through every moment of the day. He stays by our side as we sleep and can speak to us even then very powerfully, through our dreams.

Some people feel that God will only be evident in specific-ally spiritual things like church services, Bible study, preaching etc. It's true that God does use these means to speak to us, but

we only have to look at the life of Jesus and the prophets to
see that God would use anything in life and creation and any
moment in time to be a channel for His voice and presence.
Jesus experienced His Father giving Him revelation through
such mundane occurrences as a housewife losing a coin, a man
sowing his crops, a builder laying foundations, a family giving
their kids tea, a sparrow falling to the ground, a tiny wild-
flower...

The God of the Present Moment

In his book *God Is Closer Than You Think*, John Ortberg says:

> "I believe *this* can be the greatest moment of your life
> because this moment is the place where you can meet
> God. In fact, this moment is the *only* place where you can
> meet God."

John then refers to a spiritual director named Jean Pierre de
Caussade and his book *The Sacrament of the Present Moment*, in
which he says that each moment of our lives can be a
sacrament, a vehicle for God's love and power. John continues:

> "In the same way that every lungful of air gives life to our
> body, every moment in time, can, if we learn to let it, give
> life to our soul. This moment is as God filled as any we
> have ever lived."[1]

Personal Illustrations

My friend, Chris, shared with me how in a moment of time
God revealed to her that He truly existed and loved her. She
had been searching for Him for a long time and had started
attending a church, but did not know Him in a personal way.
Then she went on a retreat at a monastery (not knowing at all

what a retreat was!). There God began to make Himself
known to her. She woke suddenly one night with a line from
a hymn resounding in her mind and could not get back to
sleep until she had written it down. On the final day she
opened a Bible (a new experience for her!), then, in her own
words:

> "The Bible opened at 1 Corinthians 13, the passage on
> love. Suddenly I shot up off the bed and stood bolt
> upright. I still don't know what happened in that
> moment, but I just know in that moment, in that instant,
> I was told: there *is* a God ... that this God was within me
> and it was all about love, learning to love and learning to
> be loved. That moment was a turning point in my life. I
> had found the God I was searching for and He was a
> God that was able to communicate with me ... "[2]

In Chris's story God came to her in a moment of Spirit-
inspired revelation, using the silence of the monastery, the
words of the hymn and the Bible passage as channels for His
voice.

Now here is another example of how He came to me this
morning. My experience was totally different from Chris's. He
used a very ordinary and fun thing as a channel for His voice,
but nonetheless it had a dynamic effect. I was sitting in the
bath! I had been feeling a bit low. I thought, I wish I had more
of a sense of humour, I feel I am so boring as I never hear
people's jokes and don't really know what makes people laugh.
I said to the Lord, "Lord, can You help me develop more of a
sense of humour?"

I then lay back, shut my eyes and enjoyed the hot water.
When I opened my eyes, there was the "hippo" flannel glove
bobbing around in the bubbles next to me. I burst out
laughing because it had a smiley face and it looked for all
the world as if it was playing hide-and-seek with me in the

bubbles, smiling and winking each time it came into view. Then I gasped. How had the "hippo" come to be just there? I knew that, having finished with it earlier, I had put it up on the ledge at the opposite end of the bath. Even if it had fallen back in, it would have been trapped by my feet, not up behind my head! In that moment God spoke to me: "It doesn't matter if you can't hear others' jokes. Am I not the God of laughter and joy? If you have eyes to see, I will come to you and we will laugh together in many other 'hippo' moments!"

How Do We Know It Is God?

Following a story like that, many will ask, "But how do you know that is God speaking and not just your imagination?" The simple answer is that we never know for absolute certainty that God has spoken. That is where faith has to come in. I called my first book of this series *Expecting God to Speak to You* and that title sums up the essence of our fellowship with God. We need to *expect* that He wants to speak to us and will enable us to hear Him; having said that, there are certain pointers to discerning when it is God speaking.

For Chris, she just "knew" suddenly. A knowing that was not there before came into her heart that God was real and was love. She didn't hear any words or see any visions, she just "knew". For me it was a sudden awareness of the "hippo". As if I was seeing something so ordinary in a new way and then as I took time to look at it and focus my attention on it, I "heard" His words as thoughts that came into my mind.

I often find that my thoughts may turn in a new direction as I see an object or some part of creation and can't stop thinking about it. Or I become aware of an unexpected insight after talking to Him about a problem. I may get ideas flitting through my mind like a kite sailing across the sky. I can let them go thinking they are just my imagination or draw them in to look at them more closely. I can read a Bible passage and think, I know that, or I can read it, reflect on it and talk with Him about it and trust that the ideas and responses that come to me are being directed by His Spirit.

LIFE-CHANGING DIALOGUE

But in thinking about God speaking it is important to realize that God is a Father who wants to converse, not just "tell" us.

The verse at the start of this chapter shows how God came to Moses through something as ordinary as a bush. He then engaged Moses in a dialogue that ultimately transformed every aspect of Moses' life. Several key elements of this dialogue were as follows:

- God revealed who He was
- God made known some of His character and ways
- God made known His purposes and desires
- God affirmed Moses and told him he was chosen
- Through Moses' response, God exposed the hidden, sinful areas of Moses' life
- Moses came face to face with his own prison of fear and inadequacy
- Through God's response Moses was enabled to step out of that prison

This is the pattern that we see again and again throughout the Old Testament and in Christ's interactions with people. God speaks to us for a purpose and although He will use any moment and any thing to speak through, He never just engages in aimless chitchat!

I remember my excitement when I first got a TV that could access subtitles for the deaf. I'd never got into the soaps because I hadn't been able to follow what the characters were saying. Now at last all was about to be revealed! Excitedly I switched on *Eastenders* and settled myself down for a treat.

After a few minutes of inane and depressing conversations I said to my friend, "Are they always like this?"

"Yes, always," she laughed.

I've hardly watched another soap since!

WE NEED TO SEEK HIM

So while I have emphasized that God loves to speak to us, it is never in an aimless way and nor is He like a dog who comes eagerly running for a treat when we blow the whistle! He is God and it is awe-inspiring that He makes Himself known to us. We need to seek Him with that sense of awe and wonder, even while being confident that, as our loving Father, He delights to be with us. There will be many times when we can't sense His presence at all and He seems completely silent. But when we do meet Him then we need to take hold of it and engage with Him in the fullest way we can. Sometimes that meeting may be costly as He shows us things that we would prefer to remain hidden. But if Moses had run away from that conversation with God because it was too painful, he would not have been able to take hold of God's grace to become the man God had called him to be.

- The exodus may never have happened!
- The shape of history would have been radically different!
- Conversing with God is risky. It can have global effects!

IN HIS LOVE HE DRAWS US
TO DIALOGUE WITH HIM

This verse from the Song of Solomon shows His passion to draw us out and engage with us:

"My dove in the clefts of the rock,
  in the hiding-places on the mountainside,

show me your face,
   let me hear your voice;
for your voice is sweet,
   and your face is lovely."

(SONG OF SOLOMON 2:14)

God is calling to us as His beloved today to come out into the open and be transformed by His Spirit. As this verse shows, He calls us with tenderness and compassion. He sees exactly where we are and knows why we are there, but longs for us to come close to Him and trust in His delight in us and His desire to heal and affirm us. As we open up to His Spirit He teaches us to become aware of His presence within us and to hear His voice. As we communicate back to Him, He empowers us to be changed on the inside.

THE FIRST TIME I HEARD HIM

One of the first times the Lord spoke to me, I was in a bus shelter late at night in a furious temper! A chance remark from another student had ignited old hurts and I'd blown up. I had only been a Christian for a few months and I felt I had been deceived about God because nothing in my life had changed. On an angry impulse I ran away from college and ended up in the bus shelter determined never to go back, either to college or to God.

And He spoke to me there. I heard His voice like clear words. So clear in fact that I jumped up and said, "Pardon?"

He said, *"I love you and want to be a Father to you."*

These words were the start of my journey towards healing and transformation. They stopped me in my angry tracks. I couldn't believe He had come to me when I was so angry and bitter. When He continued speaking to me, His words came like simple thoughts in my mind. Gentle, yet life-changing. They pierced through my defences and gave me the courage to turn around and return to college and take up the reins of my new faith again. He told me that He wanted me to be like a real daughter with Him, to share my joys and my struggles, my happinesses and my hurts and that He would answer me.

What God revealed to me that night, Richard Foster describes similarly:

> "Carry on ongoing conversation with God about the daily stuff of life ... just talk to God. Share your hurts; share your sorrows; share your joys; freely and openly. God listens in compassion and love, just as we do when our children come to us. He delights in our presence. When we do this we will discover something of inestimable value. We will discover that by praying we learn to pray."[3]

Many of Us Are Hiding

Like me in that bus shelter and like the dove in the clefts of the rock, many of us are hiding. We probably won't literally crouch behind a rock like the dove! But we can bury ourselves in our activities, our work, our relationships and even our service to Him, not realizing, or not believing that the thing He most wants from us is our presence and love. Others of us deliberately hide our real selves, often because of hurt and rejection in the past. We daren't reveal our vulnerability or express our true feelings or desires. We put on a tough or humorous front or live constantly trying to serve and please others but not daring to let them reach out to us.

But always, God is calling us in love to come out of our hiding places, to face with Him the pain of exposure and so be healed.

The Message of Zacchaeus

I am always moved by the story of Zacchaeus (Luke 19:1–10). Luke describes two possible reasons why Zacchaeus chose to hide in the sycamore tree when he knew Jesus would pass by. Firstly, because he was so short and he wanted to make sure he could see over people's heads. Secondly, he was a despised chief tax collector. His exploiting of his fellow Israelites had brought him riches but also earned their hatred. So now his life was filled with the fear of exposure and judgement. Our bad choices and sinful lifestyles often act like landing pads for Satan to enter in and choke our real selves. We then become controlled by the very thing that seemed such a gain and fear grips us. Zacchaeus was pulled two ways, but his fear of the people ran even deeper than his desire to see Jesus. He wanted to see Jesus but he certainly didn't want to be seen himself. After all, this holy man would surely agree that he was despicable and only fit for condemnation!

And then came that amazing moment when Jesus stopped under the very tree where Zacchaeus was hiding. I imagine Zacchaeus quickly drawing the leaves and branches closer, nervous, yet congratulating himself on his great vantage point. No can possibly know he is there. No one will see him. Zacchaeus preens himself a little and peers down through the leaves. Is he about to see firsthand one of those miracles he's heard so much about?

"[Jesus] *looked up and said to him, 'Zacchaeus, come down immediately. I must stay at your house today.'* "

(LUKE 19:5)

I can only imagine the paralysing shock followed by the electrifying joy that swept through Zacchaeus in that instant. He was known, he had been seen. And yet, Jesus wanted to be with him! If Jesus knew Zacchaeus' name and that he was up in the tree, he certainly knew of his sinful lifestyle! And thus we see the compassionate heart of God. Jesus' thoughts were focused on Zacchaeus' need to be loved. Through those few simple words He entered with Zacchaeus into life-changing dialogue. We see the immediate effect of Jesus' words on Zacchaeus:

> "... he came down at once and welcomed him gladly ... 'Look Lord! Here and now I give half of my possessions to the poor, and if I have cheated anybody out of anything, I will pay back four times the amount.'
>
> Jesus said to him, 'Today salvation has come to this house, because this man, too, is a son of Abraham.'"
>
> (LUKE 19:6, 8–9)

YOU ARE BEAUTIFUL TO HIM AND HE WANTS TO BE WITH YOU

As that Song of Solomon verse quoted earlier expressed, God is calling you to come and be at His side. He wants to see you because *you*, as a whole person, are beautiful to Him. He wants to hear your voice because it represents all that you are, your personality, your thoughts, your joys and sadness, your opinions and desires. It is nothing to do with the externals of your physical form or the musicality of your voice. Marilyn has a beautiful singing voice while mine is abysmal! But He calls both Marilyn and me out of hiding so He can listen to us and discern our longings and respond to our prayers. To Him we are all beautiful irrespective of what we can do. We are beautiful because *He* made us and we are covered with the purity of Jesus.

BUT HOW CAN WE BE BEAUTIFUL? WE ARE SINNERS AND IT IS GOD WE NEED TO BE WORSHIPPING NOT OURSELVES!

Even as I write I can hear many of you protesting. "God is the beautiful One, not us, we're sinners! We'll get trapped in pride if we go around thinking 'I'm beautiful!'"

Try to imagine it like this:

It's as if we are a work of art that a vandal has defaced. The whole of it needs restoring. *And the only way it can truly be restored is when the Artist looks at it with eyes of love to see and recreate the beauty that He wrote into its design.*

Then with passion, perseverance and painstaking care, the Artist removes every defacing brushstroke and repairs every jagged cut and tear until the whole masterpiece is restored.

THE ONE CRUCIAL DIFFERENCE

As far as it goes, this illustration depicts God's work in restoring our lives. But there is a crucial difference. The artistic masterpiece is an inanimate recipient of both the acts of vandalism and restoration. We, however, are living beings. To varying degrees we have all colluded with the vandal in making destructive choices in our own lives and in vandalising others' lives. But like that work of art we are helpless to change ourselves although many of us spend our whole lives trying to find an answer or a magic formula to become the person we long to be.

So Jesus, the Master Artist, became the answer. The One who had made us like Himself now hung in that place of defilement and took all the ugly brush strokes, rips and rubbish into Himself. And somehow, incredibly, as He willingly allowed His own purity to be defiled in this way, He shattered the power of the vandal, broke the cycle and opened the door for us to be eternally free.

Now He comes again as the Master Artist and looks at us with eyes of love that can see past the effects of that vandalism to the beauty of His original design. Then with passion, perseverance and painstaking care, He works to restore us. But this is where our part comes in. Whereas a work of art is passive in the restoring process, Jesus gives us the choice to respond and work with Him. He offers us His own beauty, but won't force us to wear it. He desires our friendship and love. He asks us to listen to the Holy Spirit and rejoices when we see the truth about ourselves that we are forgiven and beloved by Him. And whenever we choose to agree with Him, more of those yucky brushstrokes are washed away. When we choose to listen to Him and respond to His love, it's as if the stabs that have pierced right down to the heart of our makeup are transformed into peace, compassion and joy. When we choose to see others with His artist's eyes and join Him in His restoring work in their lives, then we become the kind of masterpiece where someone only has to look at us to recognise the hand of the Artist.

AGREEING WITH WHAT HE SAYS ABOUT US: A KEY ISSUE

I believe that living in the truth of who we are in Christ is one of the key issues of our day and I would go as far as to say that until that happens the Kingdom of God will not come in its fullness! We see again and again interactions and dialogues with people in both the Old and New Testaments, where God would not let them stay in that place of feeling negative about themselves. For example, in Jeremiah:

> *"The word of the LORD came to me, saying,*
>
> *'Before I formed you in the womb I knew you,*
> *before you were born I set you apart;*
> *I appointed you as a prophet to the nations.'*
>
> *'Ah, Sovereign LORD,' I said, 'I do not know how to speak; I am only a child.'"*
>
> (JEREMIAH 1:4–6)

God initiated this conversation by communicating a truth to Jeremiah directly, Spirit to spirit. The word that came to Jeremiah fully rested on the truth as revealed in the Scriptures, but had an immediacy about it that exposed Jeremiah's feelings of inadequacy. As God continued to talk with Jeremiah His power flowed through His words to melt away Jeremiah's sense of inferiority:

> "But the LORD said to me, 'Do not say, "I am only a child." You must go to everyone I send you to ... Do not be afraid of them, for I am with you and will rescue you.' "
>
> (JEREMIAH 1:7–8)

Jeremiah's perspective changed and he was able to let go of the sense of being too young and too small to be used by God. He then started to move out prophetically, hearing the Lord's heart for the nation.

GOD'S WORD IS POWERFUL TO FREE US

God's words to Jeremiah were true and revealed the power of the lies that were controlling Jeremiah. Often these things are buried in our subconscious, but as we listen to God and respond honestly from our hearts it's as if His light exposes and destroys their strongholds.

This is because His words are full of the creative, life-giving power of the Holy Spirit. They are never, like our own, simply words that just break the silence then are gone:

> "For the word of God is living and active. Sharper than any double-edged sword, it penetrates even to dividing soul and spirit, joints and marrow; it judges the thoughts and attitudes of the heart."
>
> (HEBREWS 4:12)

A PERSONAL EXAMPLE
OF A LIFE-CHANGING DIALOGUE

The following is lifted directly from my journal. I believe this was not just for me in my situation, it is for all of us. I was going through a time of blessing in many ways and yet could not shake off a very deep sense of inner pain. I prayed about it over quite a few months and on one particular day found myself in the middle of a shattering, but ultimately life-changing conversation with God in which He lovingly exposed the root of my pain and gave me a new, true perspective on what He had done for me. I needed to live in this truth. This extract starts from the middle of these prayerful reflections with a revelation about the suicidal feelings that I'd struggled with for many years as a young adult:

> "Why am I remembering this, Lord? I feel afraid looking at this issue. I've said that I had suicidal feelings over and over in my testimony for the last eighteen years. But, this is different. Please help me, Lord. I don't want to look at this on my own. What are You saying to me about this, Lord? Come to me so that I can truly deal with it with You and be free. Please don't let me rake up things just for the sake of it and please don't let me run away if You want me to face this."

I died that you need not die

"I died that you need not die."

"I know that, Lord. I know I will be with You for eternity. I love You and am so grateful."

"But you have tried to annihilate yourself"

"That's a bit strong, Lord! There was only one really serious attempt and that was before I knew You."

"No, child, you have still tried. Not physically maybe, but in your heart. You've taken My life which I gave you that you might live fully and freely as Tracy, My beloved, and at times almost killed it."

"But how, Lord, how?"

"By the way you've squashed down what you are, denied your longings, dismissed your desires, hated your body, scorned yourself

because of your sense of inadequacy and refused to take certain steps because of your sense of failure. Each time you've done this you've been killing My life in you, trying to annihilate yourself."

"Oh, my God."

"I died to draw death in all its forms up and out of you. I became all that you were so you could become like Me; fully alive, fully whole, fully free, fully you without death in you anywhere."

"I don't understand, Lord, because last night I was meditating on those verses to do with a seed needing to fall to the ground and die to bear much fruit. Don't I *have* to deny what I am to become what You want me to be and to bear Your fruit?"

*"Child, I was the seed that fell to the ground and died so that much fruit can come. Yes, there does need to be denial but it is the old you that needs to be denied, the selfish, wounded, manipulative you, the you the devil had in his grip. Each part of **that you** I took with Me on the cross. The new you in the core of your being is the fruit. Don't ever deny that, child. Through all these years of knowing Me you have often tried to kill the new you, the fruit of My seed by denying your uniqueness and belovedness, and instead tried to resurrect and empower the old you that I have already taken. Each time you have denied yourself in this way you have mocked My death for you and given new power to the devil."*

I feel shattered by this. Never have I thought this through before. I know it is Jesus. He is grieved yet still so full of love. I don't know how to feel, I mean, I know I need to ask for forgiveness and change, but it has been me forever . . . I can sense this call to die still there inside, not physically but a sense of "I shouldn't have been me"; the feelings have never truly gone. I always buried them because I was afraid. How much more have I buried?

"Oh God, can I change? It doesn't seem enough to just say sorry. Please help me, Jesus."

Prayed Jesus would forgive me for every thought, action and imagining that has toyed with suicide.

"God help me, I don't want these old words to define and shape me any more. I want from the core of my being to know the truth that sets me free that I am Your beloved and wanted child; that I am made in Your image. I feel a war within me, but Jesus, You are with me."

Prayed He would forgive me for every way I'd internalised the negative things, for the way I mulled them over and over in my mind, for every way I've knocked myself, my longings and pushed them down. For every time I've said, "There's no point in doing that … you're silly, pathetic, boring."

Forgive me, Lord. Forgive me for thus denying what You did for me on the cross, for making it void. Forgive me, Lord, for every foothold I've given back to the devil, letting him be lord instead of You. Oh Lord, how can I change?"

"Beloved, love yourself as I love you."

"Father, you know me. Make this real, I can't do it myself. Thank You that You do embrace me, that You love me – Tracy; that I was always wanted and part of Your plan. Thank You that You made me, not my sister or anyone else I might admire and regret that I am not, but me, Trace. I accept You have now made me fully alive and You have made me unique. I accept my longings and desires, I accept my body, my mind, my understanding, my spirit and my emotional life and will are all uniquely me. In Your name I choose to love me as Tracy. Amen."

Got to rest as this has taken hours. I am exhausted, but at peace.[4]

An Exercise – a Healing Dialogue

Take some time when you can be alone with the Lord. Have some means of writing to hand.

- Thank Him that He is with you and desires to bless you and to work for the utmost good in your life. Thank Him for the gift of His Spirit and ask Him to direct your thoughts and give you His wisdom and healing through this time of dialogue. Claim His protection over your mind from all satanic confusion (Satan hates this kind of prayer as it is so powerful).

- Reflect on the examples shown in this chapter: Moses, Jeremiah, myself, each of us being real with God and "hearing" His true, life-giving replies.

- Move from your thanksgiving to a time of "chatting" with God (I always write/type this down and His responses as I go). If there is a particular struggle or worry in your heart tell Him about it. Ask Him what He thinks.

- Listen for any response and write it down. How does it make you feel? Does it give you a new perspective or sense of peace? Is it in line with Scripture and what you know of Him?

- Tell Him about your response and go on from there until you know you've reached a conclusion for now. If He has told you to do anything, e.g. to forgive someone, ask Him for His power to do it.

- Praise and thank Him for what He is showing you and doing within you.

Notes

1. John Ortberg, *God Is Closer Than You Think*, Zondervan, 2005, pp. 67–68.
2. Quoted by permission from a personal letter.
3. Richard Foster, *Prayer*, Hodder & Stoughton, 1992. p. 13.
4. The peace that I found at the end of that dialogue has never left me. Something was changed at the core of my being to do with my attitude to myself. This has been confirmed and strengthened more recently by further revelation and healing dialogue with my heavenly Father.

LEARNING GOD'S LANGUAGE

"Yet in my life, I've found something different,
My heart has been touched by a wonderful love
Deep inside I've been awakened
As if I'm hearing songs from heaven above.[1]

GOD'S LANGUAGE OF LOVE AND HEALING

Many of us carry heavy weights in our lives. Like me in the last chapter, you might feel paralysed by buried regrets and pain.
But God says to us:

"Even before he made the world, God loved us and chose us in Christ to be holy and without fault in his eyes. God decided in advance to adopt us into his own family."

(EPHESIANS 1:4–5 NLT)

"How great is the love the Father has lavished on us, that we should be called children of God! And that is what we are!"

(1 JOHN 3:1)

Verses like these form the foundations of God's heart for us. They give us faith to live in the truth of what He has made us to be. Deeper transformation comes as we open up to the Holy Spirit's work of injecting the truths of God's Word into our lives. If you find this hard to grasp, imagine a doctor's surgery; it is as if God's Word is like bottles of life-saving fluid. A tiny amount has the power to heal us, but it has to be transferred via a syringe/drip direct into our bloodstream. This is like the Holy Spirit. He injects God's powerful healing Word of truth into our lives through the medium of visions and dreams, sudden awareness or insights, people speaking God's truth to us, spiritual songs; the whole range of God's *now* language!

Our friend Lilian came from a very wounding background. Although a Christian from early childhood, the pain of her past constantly overshadowed her. She felt worthless as if a heavy weight buried her that she was powerless to shift. One day, while reading Jennifer Rees-Larcombe's book, *Turning Point*, she saw her first ever vision. She saw a set of weighing scales with heavy black coals on one side, trapping the other side full of tiny white feathers. Lilian had often felt her life was like this and was amazed that the picture was so accurate. Suddenly she saw the blood of Jesus dripping onto the feathers. The weight of the blood outweighed the coals and decisively tipped the scales the other way. Lilian knew that Jesus was telling her she was forgiven and belonged to Him and through His blood the power of the symbolic black coals of her past was broken.

God delights to speak in this way through what is often referred to as the Spiritual Gifts (see 1 Corinthians 12:1–11). These were made available to all believers through the coming of the Holy Spirit on the Day of Pentecost.

Dreams, visions and prophecy are simply a means through which God communicates to us, often to bring healing, deliverance, guidance etc.[2]

A VISION OF GOD'S FATHER HEART

God also loves to open our eyes in new ways to His character through visions and dreams.

Lilian had this kind of vision while at one of our conferences. It completely transformed her understanding of God as Father. Many of her problems had been to do with her dad. He was an aggressive and authoritarian man. He ruled with an iron fist and only spoke to crush, never to affirm his children. He was indifferent to any of her achievements or struggles. As a result Lilian could not relate to God as Father until He showed her through this vision the kind of dad *He* is.

In her own words:

"On 6th August 2003 I met Father God. I was astounded to find Him the most joyful Person, His eyes shone with merriment, they twinkled like none I have ever seen. His face was just one big smile and warmth oozed from Him.

He was so proud of us His children ... He was proclaiming me His to all of Heaven. He looked down at us and said to the angels and Jesus by His side, 'Look at them, they are Mine, aren't they great!' He said it again, 'Aren't they great!' He then encouraged me to go on doing what He had for me to do ... indicating me forward with His hand, 'You can do it, you can do it.' ...

Later that evening, once again Heaven was opened to me as we enjoyed a fun concert. They were all enjoying our fun in Heaven too. Then one of our group who had no legs and was doubled over in a wheelchair wanted to sing to Him. She chose some of Marilyn's songs. As she sang I saw tears roll down Father's cheeks and I knew it was because, despite her physical condition, she was worshipping and adoring Him. It moved Him so much.

He showed me a glimpse of Heaven because He wanted me to see just how much He cared about His children. I know now He really does love each one of us."[3]

WE NEED TO DEVELOP EYES TO SEE, EARS TO HEAR, HEARTS TO UNDERSTAND GOD'S LANGUAGE

Reading the testimony of such an encounter with God makes me long to become more fluent in His language.

When we learn a language like French we start to recognise the appropriate vocabulary, grammar and accenting until with practice we become fluent. In a similar way we need to learn God's language. Every day is full of moments and situations where God wants to draw close to us and speak into our lives. But often, because we have not learnt His language we fail to even recognise He is there or hear what He is saying. With people in a foreign country we can at least use gesture and mime to get some simple communication across, but God is hidden from our eyes. For many, this hidden nature of God is a barrier to believing in Him or accepting that He can communicate with them, but as Marilyn often laughingly says in concerts, "I can't see *you*, but you're all real, aren't you?"

In this life we can't see God with our natural eyes and mostly we can't hear Him audibly, and yet He gives us the sight and hearing we need.

NON-VISUAL AWARENESS

Knowing Marilyn has given me a lot of insight into how we can develop and use non-visual awareness. The visual land-scape that a sighted person takes for granted is missing for a blind person. If a road suddenly narrows with a tall building on the side, the sighted person automatically accommodates it in their walk. A blind person could crash into it.

And yet, when I say to Marilyn, "There's now a high wall on your right," she often says, "I know!". I say, "How do you know?" and she says, "I can hear it!" Similarly, she can hear when the wall ends and it is open space again. She will often tune into someone's sadness or happiness before any visual clues have been given or specific words spoken, through the sound of their voice. It's as if not being able to rely on sight brings the fullness of other senses alive.

I discovered this ability in myself just recently while staying at the seaside. I decided to take a night time walk down to the beach. It was pitch dark. I groped my way down the steep path holding on to the handrail. In the distance I could just make out the white of the waves as they hit the shore. With no more handrails to guide me I was truly like a blind person. I found myself becoming much more aware of the texture of the sand and stones because I was having to let my feet be my eyes.

That didn't stop me from sinking once or twice in water holes and having to flail wildly to get out again! But the closer I came to the sea, the more awed I became. I realized that the blackness was not just nothingness, but was pregnant with life and presence. I felt the cold snap of the wind on my cheeks like the touch of a person's hand, the slope of the beach was rich with messages. Whereas in daylight, I casually looked upon the whole scene and thought I knew it, now I was experiencing its different elements one after the other, a wonderful adventure of revelation. And then I arrived at the sea edge and suddenly felt such a rush of joy that I nearly knelt down in the waves! I could hear the sea! The crash of the waves, the surging of the water and roaring of the pebbles as they were pulled back into the depths, it was all clear and breathtaking. I suddenly realized I had never heard it like that before. With my deafness and tinnitus (noises in the ears) it was as if, in daylight, the sound of the waves was masked, but now without the distraction of seeing, I could hear vividly and it was so powerful that for a moment I could hardly breathe.

God spoke to me in that moment: *"You had not known the majesty of the roar of the sea until you listened with your whole being. You had not known the richness of the ground until feeling was all you could do. I am here, child, for you to discover. Enter the adventure of discovering Me in ways you had not expected. Look for Me, feel for Me, taste and smell Me close by. Listen for Me and I will reveal the majesty and gentleness of My words to you and My presence with you. In as much as the waves have always been roaring but you have only just tuned in to them, so as you choose to listen and be aware, I will enable you to suddenly tune in to Me and discover the awe and joy of realizing I have been speaking to you all along."*

THE LANGUAGE OF CREATION

Like David in Psalm 23, God was speaking to me through an intense awareness of the created world around me. For David, the experience of caring for his sheep, walking with them to ensure they had enough pasture to graze, bringing them to water so their thirst could be quenched, protecting them from wild animals ... these were all channels of awareness to him. As he performed these duties he trained his heart to be still and his spiritual ears to listen and he heard the powerful whisper of God. His work and creation itself became prophetic pictures to him of the very nature of God's loving provision and care of *His* sheep.

For David it was the hills, the streams and his work as a shepherd. With me, God was using the voice of the sea and the wind to open my spirit. As I listened I then heard those prophetic words coming clearly into my heart and mind.

Psalm 19 brings alive the spiritual reality of this experience:

> *"The heavens proclaim the glory of God.*
> *The skies display his craftsmanship.*

Day after day they continue to speak;
  night after night they make him known."

(Psalm 19:1–2 NLT)

But it is possible to be in the midst of creation and be too self-absorbed to sense God's presence. God looks for those who have "ears to hear" and hearts to seek Him. Will we be like Martha in Luke 11, so busy, even in our service to Him, that we are full of worry and distractions? Or like her sister Mary who chose to put cultural pressures aside in order to relish the treasure of Jesus' presence with her?

An Exercise to Tune into His Voice Through Creation

Put everything aside that you have on your to do list and give yourself a realistic period of time, e.g. 15–30 minutes that can just be for you and Him.

- Pray a simple prayer: "Lord, I want to share this time with You. Thank You that You want to share it with me. Open my spirit so I can become aware You are with me. Help me to hear Your voice of love as I enjoy Your creation. Amen."
- Now go for a walk. (If this is difficult for you because of disability or dependants, see if you can sit with something beautiful like a flower arrangement, a leafy plant, a window overlooking a garden or sit in the garden itself if possible. Alternatively, find a lovely picture, sculpture, candle, or spend time just looking at your baby/child/pet etc., while they are sleeping.)
- Using the walk suggestion (but adapting it to whatever you have chosen to do), take a few moments to just be still. Feel the air in your hair, the sun or rain on your cheeks, the ground under your feet. What do they feel like? What

messages do they bring you? Take time to sniff. What can you smell? Fragrances of flowers? Fumes of traffic? Food smells from restaurants? Lick your lips. Can you taste anything? Close your eyes and listen. What can you hear? Are you more aware of any particular sounds? What messages do they bring you?

- Walk along slowly, giving yourself time to be aware of the feel of the ground under your feet, the feel of your body as you move. Look, listen, touch ... stop at anything that takes your notice. Remember, Jesus is walking with you. Talk with Him about anything that strikes your attention: e.g. my sudden awareness of the majestic sound of the waves. Become aware of any emotional responses in your heart, e.g. joy, sadness, peace, stress, longing, grief, anger, worship ... and tell Him about them. Listen for any thoughts that come back to you.

- Spend as much time as you want to just enjoy being with Him and being aware of what is around you and your present experience of it. Thank Him that He made it in love. Thank Him that He is speaking to you through it and has been enjoying it with you.

- If you keep a journal take a few minutes afterwards to record what the experience meant and anything the Lord said to you. (It was as I did this after my beach experience that the prophetic word crystallised and became real to me. Up until then, it had been a jumble of powerful impressions in my mind. Now I can have the joy of recalling it whenever I want to.)

AWAKENED HEARTS

In Marilyn's song quoted at the start of the chapter, she says, *"Deep inside I've been awakened, as if I'm hearing songs from heaven above..."*[4]

When God comes to us by His Holy Spirit and brings

revelation of His presence it's as if a light goes on inside us. Something comes alive! We suddenly *know* things we were not aware of, or become aware of the beauty of Jesus in someone. We may find a new desire and ability to reach out with His love and forgiveness, or that the Bible becomes rich with meaning or we are empowered to truly offer ourselves to Him in worship.

All this is a result of the Holy Spirit's presence in our lives, but just as we learn to be aware of our bodily messages, e.g. sleepiness, or a rumbling tummy, so we need to become aware of any particular way the Holy Spirit is awakening us. The story of the two disciples that met with the risen Jesus on the road to Emmaus wonderfully illustrates how God is often close by, speaking words that will guide and transform us, yet it is possible to fail to recognise Him and miss what He is doing.

"Jesus himself came up and walked along with them; but they were kept from recognising him.

He asked them, 'What are you discussing together as you walk along?'

They stood still, their faces downcast ... Cleopas asked him, 'Are you only a visitor to Jerusalem and do not know the things that have happened there in these days ... About Jesus of Nazareth?'

He said to them, 'How foolish you are, and how slow of heart to believe all that the prophets have spoken! Did not the Christ have to suffer these things and then enter his glory?' And beginning with Moses and all the Prophets, he explained to them what was said in all the Scriptures concerning himself.

As they approached the village ... they urged him strongly, 'Stay with us' ... So he went in to stay with them.

When he was at the table with them, he took bread, gave thanks, broke it and began to give it to them. Then their eyes were opened and they recognised him, and he disappeared from their

sight. They asked each other, 'Were not our hearts burning within
us while he talked with us on the road and opened the Scriptures
to us?'"

(LUKE 24:15–19, 25–32)

Jesus had been with the disciples for three years and had
told them repeatedly that He would die and rise again. They
had witnessed Lazarus raised from the dead and other
countless miracles, yet it was as if they were deaf and blind
and nothing had penetrated their innermost understanding.
Now He had been murdered and they were devastated. The
women's excited news that He was alive simply fuelled their
grief, rather than igniting their faith. They were so caught
up in the "fact" of their anguish that something within them
gave up. It was at that point of running away from everything
they had hoped for and believed in, that Jesus came and
walked alongside them, although they did not realize it was
Him.

What Keeps Us from Recognising Jesus?

The passage says that they were *"kept from recognising him"*
and their faces were downcast. This gives me the impression
they were so bowed down by their negative perceptions
that they literally could not look up into His face. They had
also been talking together about everything. There is a fine
dividing line between being able to safely express the depth of
our pain with others and being so consumed by it that we
refuse to let Jesus give us a new perspective.

There is no one who understands our griefs more than
Jesus. He experienced the agony of rejection and betrayal in
His own life and then on the cross willingly carried the weight
of all our sorrows in order that their power to cripple us would
be broken. As was shown in this story, He is never distant in
our sufferings, but comes and walks alongside us and enters

into our pain. The shortest sentence in the Bible is the most profound:

"Jesus wept."

(JOHN 11:35)

In that moment of weeping, Jesus showed what true compassion is. He is not a Job's comforter who kicks us when we are down. Compassion means "suffer with"! Jesus felt the agony of loss and hopelessness in Lazarus' family and friends and He wept with them, sharing their pain, even while knowing that He was about to restore their joy.

Paul describes the character of God in 2 Corinthians:

"Praise be to the God and Father of our Lord Jesus Christ, the Father of compassion and the God of all comfort, who comforts us in all our troubles, so that we can comfort those in any trouble with the comfort we ourselves have received from God."

(2 CORINTHIANS 1:3–4)

Paul discovered that God is so full of compassion and comfort that it leaks from Him. And it is so real that it enables Paul to relax and to feel safe while at the same moment freeing him to do and be things he could never have imagined, like giving that same comfort and compassion to others. What is the nature of this comfort that Father God gives us? The significant word in this verse is *all*. God comes to us in *all* our moments of grief, helplessness, fear and despair and offers us true comfort. True because it is not just empty words but something that is real and heart changing.

A PROPHETIC WORD FOR SOMEONE READING THIS NOW

I believe that as someone is reading these words right now, Jesus is drawing alongside you in the same way He drew alongside those bewildered and grief-stricken disciples. You too have experienced a loss that has bewildered you in its suddenness. You feel devastated and anchorless, as if all you have trusted in and lived for has been stripped away. Words of intended comfort from others have just fuelled your grief and you are running away, in your heart if not literally.

But Jesus is with you. He has seen your grief and weeps with you. He did not let those two disciples run away and He will not let you. He listened to them share their grief with Him and He wants to listen to you if only you will open up to Him. He says: *"Beloved child, I am with you. I love you and I understand. Let me grieve with you and then warm your heart with the comfort of My presence, and the truth of My understanding. Let Me open your eyes to the many ways I want to be with you. Let Me give you My strength to turn around from the paralysis of despair and discover the joy of My purpose for you."*[5]

THE POWER OF CHOOSING TO HOLD ON TO JESUS

Once the two disciples consciously started to listen to Jesus, even though they didn't know who He was, the crippling power of their despair was broken. They said afterwards, *"Were not our hearts burning within us while he ... opened the Scriptures to us?"* He was still hidden from them, yet now there was a heart awakening, so much so that they pleaded with Him to stay with them when they reached their village.

This was the Holy Spirit, stirring up a hunger within them to be with Jesus. The Spirit is always working to bring us, the cherished Bride to her Bridegroom. He will reveal the Bridegroom to us, often after we have actually been with Him without realizing it! He will open our eyes to see Him and love Him and want to live for Him.

For the disciples the moment of revelation came as Jesus took the bread and broke it and went to pass it to them.

Suddenly there was recognition. I can only imagine the joy they must have felt as this ordinary moment of eating bread was transformed.

A Personal Moment of Revelation

I had a similar experience while on the retreat mentioned earlier. I had been struggling for a long time with some very deep-rooted feelings of failure. Now it seemed as if God was opening my eyes to recognise His loving presence with me in all kinds of unexpected ways. One of these occasions was in the dining room. Soup was served at lunchtime. We collected our food and took it over to the dining tables in silence (it was a silent retreat). My problem was that I could not balance the soup! The bowl was wide and shallow, I took two steps and knew it was going to spill! I could not call for help as we were meant to be silent and I felt embarrassed anyway (the old accusing voices of shame). Then one of the ladies on the retreat came over and carried the soup for me. She was completely relaxed about it and so I relaxed too! The next day she came up to me while I was in the lunch queue and mimed carrying my soup. As I looked at the kind twinkle in her eye I was suddenly very moved and nearly burst into tears! Every day after that either Sue or one of the others carried my soup for me, and each time I felt warmed and emotionally close to tears.

I wrote in my journal:

"I don't normally cry. Always find it hard. Got so used to burying my feelings it became part of my makeup. Now it seems the smallest things are moving me to tears ... Sue's offers to carry the soup for me each day. She does it with such kindness. There isn't any message in it that I am failing, no message of exasperation, just someone looking out for me, knowing it's an area of difficulty. Can I accept all this is You, Lord? Lord I am amazed. It *is*

You loving me through Sue and the soup. You are saying 'Am I not the God of loving kindness and tender mercy?' Thank You Lord, thank You that You come to heal me through such a simple gesture of kindness and something as ordinary as a bowl of soup."

So What Is God's Language?

Scripture

To those grieving disciples Jesus spoke from the Scriptures and opened their eyes to see Him through the meal they were sharing. His language here was His Word, written on their hearts by the Holy Spirit.

Creation and everyday life

As shown earlier in this chapter, God speaks through all He has made and through all the elements of our everyday lives

A person's actions

In my retreat experience, God's language was a person's kindness in an ordinary moment of the day.

Preaching

We may find our hearts are awakened by something a preacher says. My friend Jenny experienced this at a time when she was trying to dance in worship but often felt too silly or self-conscious. She went to a worship conference where the speaker, Roger Forrester, spoke about God being a God of dance and every day we can discover what song and dance the Trinity is doing and then join in with it. Through these words Jenny felt a warmth of recognition. In her own words: "This was just so fantastic for me because I saw it as revelation. I felt it, I agreed with it and immediately started doing it ... Every day I wake up and ask Father, 'What song and dance are You doing so I can join in?' It always brings a smile to my face. I then just move and dance, I allow God to give me a song or dance … It has revolutionised my spiritual life. It draws me straight into the spiritual realm. Even writing about it gives me peace and a smile!"

A nudging to do something

In 1981, a friend, Diana, had just arrived at an International Bible Training Institute conference when she heard of a little boy who had lost his £8 holiday spending money on his way there. Diana felt a nudging inside to give his mum, a single lady, the missing money. The mum was very grateful and later gave Diana some Bible verses that she felt God had put on her heart for her. One of the verses said, *"You shall bear fruit out of your own womb."* What the mum did not know was that Diana was having medical problems conceiving, but was desperate to have a child. Diana told her how meaningful this verse was and the lady prayed in detail for God to heal Diana and for Diana to be able to have a child of her own. Diana left believing the Lord would answer this prayer and felt like she was "walking on air". Within two months she was pregnant with her first child!

The voice of God, visions and the gifts of the Spirit

In her book, *The Shaming of the Strong*, Sarah Williams describes how she was devastated by the news at a routine scan that her longed for and expected baby was so deformed she could not possibly live after birth. Sarah was offered an immediate termination, but as she and her husband Paul prayed in their despair God revealed His broken heart of love to them:

"I can only say that we felt God the Father speak a message to our hearts as clearly as if He had been talking to us in person. 'Here is a sick and dying child. Will you love it for Me and care for it until it dies?'

With these words God gave us a taste of His heart ... for Him it was not a question of abstract ethical principal but the gentle imperative of His overwhelming love for this tiny, deformed, helpless baby ... As I lay down in my bed that night I realized the decision had already been made and I was at peace ... "

Despite the peace of their decision to carry the baby, named Cerian (meaning "Loved One"), to term, Sarah and Paul still had to live with the day-to-day agony of what was happening. Grief came to them both in different ways. While Sarah could welcome and protect Cerian's growing life within her, Paul felt distanced and grieved that he would never be able to bond with his daughter. Then one night God gave him a dream:

"He had been crying. 'I saw the baby in my dream (Paul said). She was about three or four years old. Her hair was long. She was running fast through an open field towards the mountains. She was so free.' He added quietly, 'I feel connected with her now.'"

One of the hardest moments for Sarah was in the throes of labour. Her body knew it was time for Cerian to leave, but that would mean losing her. Emotionally Sarah just couldn't do it. The pain and fear were overwhelming. She prayed in desperation for Jesus to help her:

"Then quite suddenly into my mind came the image ... of a rider on a great, black stallion at full gallop. There was sound, movement and power in the sight ... The mane streamed and the hair of the rider was full of sweat and rain. I knew then that it was Jesus. He was riding towards me with incredible urgency. He was coming for Cerian. The sheer energy of the image stilled my sobbing.

The rider was both warrior and lover, frantic for His loved one, coming to rescue her..."[6]

Ask the Holy Spirit to be your language teacher!

Have you felt inspired by these stories and illustrations of the many ways God speaks to us and the depth of healing and transformation He brings as we respond? Learning His language is an adventure that He enjoys with each of us. He wants us to experience more and more that moment of joy and awe when we suddenly recognise Him or find He is giving us His thoughts and understanding. He wants our openness to the Holy Spirit and our expectation that He knows how to touch and help us. Jesus said we just need to be as simple as a little child asking his Daddy for food (see Matthew 7:7–16). Then our heavenly Father will give us all we need to hear and know Him.

A "LITTLE CHILD" EXERCISE AND PRAYER

Take a few moments to still your heart.

- Say hello to Jesus/Father God
- Use something like this simple prayer to tell Him you want to learn His language:

> "Thank You that You want to talk to me and that You give me Your Holy Spirit to teach me how to hear You. I really want to learn Your language! Please help me be open to You, dear Holy Spirit. I want to see You, to hear You, to love You and grow deeper in understanding You. You know the things I struggle with, the hurts, fears and confusions. Please speak to me in such a way that I am healed and changed and become more and more like You. Thank You Daddy. Amen."

- Recall some of the ways I listed earlier that He speaks through. As you continue with your day, reach out to Him from your heart. Let your awareness of Him be like an antenna tuning in to the radio waves. Is He giving you a nudging of His presence through anything you are looking at or thinking about? Do you have a phrase or visual idea keep coming to your mind? Do you sense Him close in any particular moment, person or activity?
- Talk to Him about these nudgings and ask Him to make them clearer to you.
- Make a note in your journal of anything that has come to you or any dialogue you have had with Him and thank Him for it.

In Conclusion

I believe it is God's greatest joy to meet with us, His beloved children and fill our lives and hearts with His love. Out of Paul's own life-changing experiences of encountering God and learning to live in step with Him, he prayed this prayer for us all:

> *"I pray that out of his glorious riches he may strengthen you with power through his Spirit in your inner being, so that Christ may dwell in your hearts through faith. And I pray that you, being rooted and established in love, may have power ... to grasp how wide and long and high and deep is the love of Christ, and to know this love that surpasses knowledge – that you may be filled to the measure of all the fullness of God."*
>
> (Ephesians 3:16–19)

It's my prayer that having read this book that you will be helped and inspired to go further on your own journey with God, knowing He is with you every step of the way. May you know ever more deeply the wonder and joy of meeting with

Him, hearing His healing words of love and engaging in life-changing encounters with Him.

Notes

1. A verse from "Seeing Is Believing" from *Overflow of Worship* by Marilyn Baker, © 1998 Marilyn Baker Music, Kingsway/ThankYou Music.
2. For more understanding regarding the Spiritual Gifts, you may like to read my book *Letting God Speak Through You*, New Wine Press, 2006.
3. Used by permission.
4. "Seeing Is Believing" from *Overflow of Worship* by Marilyn Baker, © 1998 Marilyn Baker Music, Kingsway/ThankYou Music.
5. This word of knowledge and prophetic word of comfort came to me very powerfully as I was meditating on and writing about the Scripture passage. If you know it applies to you, please don't dismiss it. Take it to heart and receive the comfort and help Jesus is offering you. He knew you would be reading this even before the book was finished and submitted to the publisher!
6. Sarah Williams, *The Shaming of the Strong*, Kingsway Communications Ltd., 2005, pp. 30, 64–65, 122–123.

About the Author

Tracy Williamson was born in 1964 in North East London. At the age of two she became ill with encephalitis, which left her deaf and partially sighted with coordination difficulties. The hearing loss was not fully discovered until Tracy was twelve, which meant that she was often thought to be a slow learner. When Tracy was seven, her father died of cancer. Soon a new father came into the family. He turned out to be a violent-tempered man who had a damaging effect throughout Tracy's teen years. These childhood traumas had a huge negative impact on Tracy's life and she became very introverted and depressed. Despite that and her deafness, she pushed forward in her academic achievements, becoming a wide reader and gaining GCSE and A-Levels, excelling in English. When she was eighteen, she was offered a place at what is now Hertfordshire University to take a teaching degree in the hope of becoming a teacher of the deaf. Tracy's first year at college was fraught as she came to realize that she couldn't leave her past behind. She also learned she would find teaching too stressful because of her deafness.

After a long period of anguished soul-searching, Tracy made the decision to give up her dream of teaching the deaf and transferred to a BA Degree in English Literature and Education. This whole process made her desperate for real answers and help in her life and after many conversations with

Christian fellow students she became a Christian in June 1983. Tracy then went on to complete her degree, gaining a 2.1 (Hons.) in June 1985.

MINISTRY

In that same year, prior to forging a career with the visually impaired, Tracy met with blind singer/songwriter Marilyn Baker and a deep bond of friendship formed between them. Marilyn's assistant left in January 1986 and Marilyn asked Tracy to help her out temporarily. It soon became apparent however, that God was calling Tracy to the ministry and she gave up her proposed course to become Marilyn's personal assistant in April 1986. She is still in this ministry today.

TRACY'S ROLE

Initially Tracy's main role was to be a practical support and administrative assistant to Marilyn. However, it soon became clear that God had anointed Tracy with gifts of communication. Beginning with sharing her testimony in concerts, Tracy then began to receive prophetic words for individuals and churches. As her prophetic gifting developed, Tracy realized how few people expected God to speak to them personally. This led to her volunteering to do a workshop on listening to God at a conference led by Jennifer Rees-Larcombe in 1993. The workshop was a great success and ultimately led to the publication of her first book *The Voice of the Father* which was published by Hodder and Stoughton in 1996. Since then Tracy has written a number of articles promoting Marilyn's albums for various Christian publications. She has also written for Scripture Union's Bible reading notes series *Closer to God*, including a series on "The Father Heart of God" in 2001 and on the book of 2 Timothy in 2004. Her first book in this series, *Expecting God to Speak to You!*, was released in 2005. Her second book, *Letting God Speak Through You*, was published in 2006. Tracy now regularly teaches at workshops, church weekends and conferences that she and Marilyn lead together. Some of the areas she teaches on are: prophetic prayer and ministry; listening to God; prophetic evangelism; intimacy with God; the Father heart of God; breaking out of loneliness; overcoming fear and anxiety, and becoming the true Body of Christ.

FOR FURTHER
INFORMATION

If you would like information about Tracy Williamson or Marilyn Baker Ministries, please contact:

Marilyn Baker Ministries
PO Box 393
Tonbridge
Kent
TN9 9AY

Tel: 08707 501720
email: info@marilynbakerministries.org

or visit the web site:

www.marilynbakerministries.org

BY THE SAME AUTHOR

Expecting God to Speak to You!
ISBN 978 1 903725 41 2
96 pages, £5.99

Letting God Speak Through You
ISBN 978 1 903725 49 8
96 pages, £5.99

We hope you enjoyed reading this New Wine book.
For details of other New Wine books and
a range of 2,000 titles from other
Word and Spirit publishers visit our website:
www.newwineministries.co.uk